Speaking of People Intro
Peter Vincent
Alan Meadows
Naoko Nakazato
NAN'UN-DO

Speaking of People *Intro*

人とつながる英語コミュニケーション

Download Audio

音声ファイル
無料 DL
のご案内

このテキストの音声を無料で視聴（ストリーミング）・ダウンロードできます。自習用音声としてご活用ください。
以下のサイトにアクセスしてテキスト番号で検索してください。

https://nanun-do.com　テキスト番号［ **512210** ］

※ 無線 LAN（WiFi）に接続してのご利用を推奨いたします。

※ 音声ダウンロードは Zip ファイルでの提供になります。
お使いの機器によっては別途ソフトウェア（アプリケーション）の導入が必要となります。

Read by

Hannah Grace
Chris Koprowski

※ Speaking of People Intro 音声ダウンロードページは以下の QR コードからもご利用になれます。

Preface

Welcome to *Speaking of People Intro*, a textbook written for Japanese students of English who are interested in talking about people. The text is designed for active communication with many fun activities and role plays. It contains various speaking, listening, reading, and writing activities, all with colorful illustrations to help you understand and communicate about people. The textbook includes practice in such things as describing physical appearance, personality, feelings, and experiences.

In order to make the most of this textbook, we would like you to remember one thing: Don't be afraid of making mistakes. Making mistakes and learning from them is how you improve your English skills, so please try your best.

We very much enjoyed writing this textbook and hope that you have an equally enjoyable time talking about people in English.

Speaking of Peopleにようこそ。本書は人について話すことに興味のある日本人学生のために書かれました。このテキストには、コミュニケーションを活発に行えるような多様なアクティビティとロールプレイが盛り込まれています。スピーキング、リスニング、ライティングタスクなどをカラフルなイラストで表現し、人に関する様々なコミュニケーションに役立つアクティビティにしました。その中には、身体的な特徴、性格、感情や経験などを表す練習が含まれています。 本書を最も有効に活用してもらうために、一つメッセージがあります。間違いを恐れないでください。間違いから学ぶことが英語のスキルを上達させることにつながります。恥ずかしがらず、思い切ってトライしてください。

著者一同にとって、本書を書くことは非常に楽しいプロセスでした。みなさんも、本書を使って人に関する様々な話題を英語で楽しめるようになってほしいと思います。

Peter Vincent（Seitoku University）
Alan Meadows（Seitoku University）
Naoko Nakazato（Seitoku University）

CONTENTS

Classroom English
教室で使う英語

Try to speak as much English as you can in class.
クラス内ではできるだけ英語で話しましょう。

02

Here are some expressions you might need to use.
以下の表現を参考にしてください。

1. May I ask a question? 質問してもよいですか
2. Could you repeat that, please? もう一度言ってもらえますか。
3. Could you speak more slowly, please? もっとゆっくり言ってもらえますか。
4. How do you spell ________ ? ________ はどのようにつづりますか。
5. What does ________ mean? ________ はどういう意味ですか。
6. How do you say ________ in English? ________ 英語でどう言いますか。
7. OK, I understand. はい、わかります。

And here are some expressions your teacher might say:
先生は以下の表現を使うかもしれません。

1. Please repeat. 繰り返してください。
2. Please answer the question. 質問に答えてください。
3. Please open your books. 本を開けてください。
4. Please close your books. 本を閉じてください。
5. Work in pairs / Work with a partner. パートナーと行ってください。
6. Look at page ________. ________ ページを見てください。
7. Do you understand? わかりますか？

Unit 1
Introductions
自己紹介

Speaking スピーキング

Practice the following dialogues with a partner. After you have practiced the model conversation a few times, substitute the underlined information with the words in the boxes.
以下の会話をパートナーと練習してください。数回練習したら、下線の部分を枠内の表現に言いかえて再度練習しください。

Study Tip: Don't just read the dialogues. Try to maintain eye contact with your partner while speaking.
キーポイント：ただ会話を読むだけでなく、パートナーの顔をきちんと見て話しましょう。

Dialogue 1 会話1 03

James: My name's James Morgan. (It's) Nice to meet you.(1)

Emi: I'm Emi Nakamura. (It's) Nice to meet you,(1) too.
Are you a university* student?

James: Yes, I am. I go to City University. I'm a senior.*(2)
How about you?

Emi: I'm a student, too. I go to Southern University.
I'm a junior.*(2)

1. (I'm) Pleased to meet you. (It's) Good to meet you.	2. freshman* sophomore*

Dialogue 2 会話2 04

James: I study economics*. What do you study, Emi?

Emi: (I study) Childhood education*.

James: Oh, really? Do you want to be a teacher in the future?

Emi: Yes, I do. I want to work in a kindergarten.*(1) How about you, James?

James: I want to work in a bank.*(2)

Emi: Oh, really?

1. an elementary school.*	2. computer company

* university 大学　senior 大学4年生　junior 大学3年生　freshman 大学1年生　sophomore 大学2年生
economics 経済　childhood education 児童教育　kindergarten 幼稚園　bank 銀行
elementary school 小学校

Culture Note

Names, Titles, and the Way We Address Others

英語の名前、敬称、呼び方について

- Names: In English, the first name comes first and the last name, or family name, comes last.
  英語の名前：last name は姓、first name は名です。このように通常英語では、下の名前を先に、姓をあとに表します。Walt Disney の名は Walt、姓は Disney ですよね。

- Titles: When you address someone with courtesy or respect, add Mr./Mrs./Miss/Ms. before their last name.
  英語の敬称：「〜さん」と丁寧に呼びたいときは、Mr. や Mrs. Miss Ms. などの敬称のあとに姓（last name）を付けて呼びます。　✕ Mr. Paul　○ Mr. Jackson

- Mr. = Married or single man　既婚・未婚の男性
  Ms. = Married or single woman　既婚・未婚の女性
  Mrs. = Married woman　既婚の女性
  Miss = Single woman　未婚の女性

- Calling teachers: You should not call your teacher "Teacher!" At university, you can call your teacher with respect using "Professor + last name" or "Mr./Mrs./Miss/Ms. + last name."
  先生を呼ぶとき：先生を、"Teacher!" とは呼べません。大学では先生に呼びかける時は、"Professor + last name"、あるいは "Mr./Mrs./Miss/Ms. + last name" で先生を呼びます。

▶Practice 1 Matching: Names 名前の呼び方

Put the correct letter in the space to match the explanation on the right.

1. から 8. の名前の説明として適切なものを A ～ H から選びましょう。

______ 1. Yuka Tanaka

______ 2. Emi

______ 3. Smith

______ 4. Miss Gandhi

______ 5. Mrs. Ito

______ 6. Ms. Janis Cooper

______ 7. Mr. Ivan O'Brian

______ 8. Professor Li

A. Last name

B. A man or woman who teaches at a university

C. A single* woman

D. A married* woman

E. Full name (with no title*)

F. A woman who may be single or married

G. First name

H. A man who may be single or married

▶Practice 2 Reading リーディング 🎧05

Listen to the self-introduction. Then answer the questions.

以下の自己紹介を聞いて、Candice についての質問に答えましょう。

Hello, everyone. I'm Candice Lin. I'm Canadian. I live in Vancouver. I'm 18 years old and I'm a university student. I go to the University of British Columbia. I study business. I want to be a businessperson* in the future. I live with my family. There are three people in my family. I like to read in my free time. I also like to play tennis. In the future*, I want to start my own company. Thank you.

Answer the following questions using full sentences.

以下の質問に完全な文で答えましょう。

Example: How old is she? She is 18 years old.

Questions:

1. What is her name? ______________________________
2. Where does she live? ______________________________
3. What does she study? ______________________________
4. What does she do in her free time? ______________________________

* single 独身 married 既婚 title 肩書き businessperson 会社員 future 将来

Grammar* 1

06

Subject Pronouns 主語代名詞（I, You, He, She など）

One person 1人

Two or more people 2人以上

<table>
<tr><td>I'm ...
(I am ...)</td><td rowspan="3">... Japanese.
... 19 years old.
... a university student.</td><td>We're ...
(We are ...)</td><td rowspan="3">... Australian.
... 18 years old.
... university students.</td></tr>
<tr><td>You're...
(You are ...)</td><td>You're...
(You are ...)</td></tr>
<tr><td>He's/She's ...
(He/She is ...)</td><td>They're ...
(They are ...)</td></tr>
</table>

One thing 1個

Things 2個以上

It's ... (It is ...)	... big. ... a cute toy.	They're (They are ...)	... modern. ... tall buildings.

▶Practice 3 Pronouns 代名詞

Put the correct pronoun from Grammar 1 above in the spaces below.

Grammar 1 から正しい代名詞を選んで空欄に記入しましょう。

My name is Mark Jenner. ______________ am a university student. My best friend is Jon. ______________ is also a student. ______________ go to the same university together. I like my university, because ______________ is big and beautiful. The classrooms are very nice, because ______________ are new and clean. I like my teachers, too, because ______________ are interesting.

* grammar 文法

Grammar 2

"Be" and Other Verbs (be 動詞と一般動詞の使い分け)

be 動詞を使うとき

★ When we want to say "A = B", we use a "be" verb.
"A は B です" と言いたいときに be 動詞を使えます。

I ***am*** 21 years old.　私＝ 21 才
A　　　B

Is he the manager?　彼＝マネジャー
A　　　B

質問文をつくるときは、肯定文の主語と be 動詞の順番を入れ替え、否定文は be 動詞に not を付けます。
He ***is*** a student. → ***Is*** he a student?
He ***is*** a student. → He ***is not*** a student.

★ You may think that the Japanese *wa* and *ga* are equivalent to the English "be" verb. Well, that is not the case. The meaning of the "be" verb is "to be" and "to exist." Japanese *desu* and *de aru* / *de iru* would be the appropriate equivalent in meaning. Also, Japanese sentence structure is different from that of English, so you can not translate it according to the order of Japanese sentence structure.

be 動詞 (is, am, are) は、日本語の「〜は」や「〜が」に相当すると思っていませんか？実は、そうではないのです！ここで使われる be 動詞は、「〜である / いる」という「存在する」という意味です。また、英文は日本語の語順と同じ順序では訳せません。
John is a teacher. → John（ジョン） × is（は） a teacher（先生）
John（ジョンは） ○ is（である） a teacher（先生）

注：この文中の "John" は、「John」ではなく、「John は」です！

動詞の現在形を使うとき

（質問文に主語の前に do / does、否定文は動詞の前に don't / doesn't を付ける）

★ The present tense is used to describe actions that happen regularly or habitually.
I wash my hair every day.　髪は毎日洗うよ（普段やっていること、習慣）

普段やっていること、習慣を表す

★ The present tense is also used to give information about a state.
He doesn't have a textbook.　彼、テキスト持ってないんだ（状態）

状態を表す

★ The present tense is used to express a fact without any time reference or to state the rules of nature and the way the world is.
Mike speaks four languages.　Mike は4か国語しゃべるの
It snows a lot in Hokkaido.　北海道は冬すごい雪ふるよ（事実）

時制に関係のない事実、法則を表す

▶Practice 4 Writing: Yes / No Questions ライティング：Yes / No の質問

Look at Practice 2, Candice's self-introduction, on page 8. Answer the following questions in full sentences. Notice that answers to questions that begin with a verb should usually begin with "Yes" or "No." If the answer is "No," write the correct answer.

P. 8 の Practice 2 の Candice の自己紹介を見て質問に完全な文で答えましょう。動詞（is, am, are, do, does）で始まる質問文には、Yes/No で答えます。"No" で答える時は正しい答えも書きましょう。

Example:

Questions	Yes / No answers
Is Candice Canadian?	Yes, she is.
Does she live in Montreal?	No, she does not. She lives in Vancouver.

Questions **Yes / No answers**

1. Is Candice 18 years old? ______________________________
2. Is she a university student? ______________________________
3. Does she study history? ______________________________
4. Does she have three people in her family? ______________________________
5. Does she want to be a singer in the future? ______________________________
6. Does she like to play online games in her free time? ______________________________
____
7. Does she want to start her own company in the future? ______________________________

Grammar 3

07

Questions Starting with "Wh" and "How"

"Wh" と "How" ではじまる疑問文

You can't answer these questions with "Yes" or "No."
以下の質問文には Yes/No では答えられません。

What's (What is) your name?	My name is Richard Blake.
What does she do?*	She's a teacher.
What do they study?	They study business.
Where do you live?	I live in Osaka.
How old is he?	He's 20 years old.
What do you do in your free time?	I watch TV and read.*
What's (What is) your future dream?	I want to travel to many countries.

* "What does she do?" is a question that asks what someone's job is. When you are asked "What do you do?" you can say what kind of work you do, or whether you are a student. If you ask "What do you do every day?" you are asking about someone's "routine" not their job.

What does she do? は、職業を聞く特別な表現です。What do you do? と聞かれたらあなたの職業（ビジネスマン、学生など）を答えましょう。「普段何をするのか？」と聞いているのではありません。でもこの文に "every day" を入れると、「彼女って毎日何してるんだろうね？」という、普段の行動について聞く文になります。

* "read" by itself could mean "read books," so if that is what you mean, you do not need to add books at the end.

"read" だけで、本を読むという意味にもなるので、あとに "books" と入れる必要はありません。

▶Practice 5 Matching: Wh / How Questions Wh / How を使った質問

Put the correct letters for the answers in the spaces.

1～6の質問の答えとして適切なものを、A～Fの中から選びましょう。

____	1. Where does Candice come from?	A. 18 years old.
____	2. Where does she live?	B. Business.
____	3. How old is she?	C. Read and play tennis.
____	4. What does she study?	D. Start her own company.
____	5. What does she do in her free time?	E. She lives in Vancouver.
____	6. What does she want to do in the future?	F. Canada.

Now take turns asking and answering the questions in pairs.

▶Practice 6 Writing ライティング

Look at Practice 2, Candice's self-introduction, on page 8. Write answers in full sentences to the questions below. The first one has been done for you.

P. 8 の Practice 2 の Candice の自己紹介を読み、以下の質問に完全な文で答えましょう。1. は例です。

1. Where does Candice live?

   She lives in Vancouver. ________________________________

2. What does she do?

   ____

3. How old is she?

   ____

4. What does she study?

   ____

5. What does she like to do in her free time?

   ____

6. What does she want to do in the future?

   ____

▶Practice 7 Listening リスニング 08

Listen to the introduction and write in the missing words

以下の自己紹介を聞いて空欄を埋めましょう。

______________, everybody. ______________ Naoki Kitagawa. __________ a university student and I study nursing. I want to be a nurse ________________. I'm ________________. I live in Yokohama with ______________. There are many fun things to do in Yokohama. In ________________, I like to ____________________ and ______________. I also ______________ go to coffee shops and talk ____________________. There are only ______________ in my family, my mother, father, ______________.

Grammar 4

09

Possessive Pronouns

所有代名詞

Singular 単数（一人*、一個）

* ここでは “Your” は、「あなたの」

～の（～の持っている、～に属する）

My ***My*** name is David.
Your How do you spell ***your*** name?
His/Her/Its I am ***her*** friend.

Plural 複数（二人*、二個以上）

* ここでの ”Your” は、「あなた方の」2 人以上

Our These are ***our*** textbooks.
Your Please open ***your*** textbooks.
Their Is ***their*** hometown Osaka?

Note

代名詞には、以下４つの使い方があります。“I, my, me, mine / you, your, you, yours… ♪ ” というように、覚えた順番で思い出すのではなく、必ず文の意味を理解して使い方を練習しましょう！

1. I, you, he, she, it, we, they 「～は」という意味。主語になる。
   He and I are friends. 彼と私は友達です

2. my, your, his, her, its, our, their 「～の」という意味。
   Our teacher is Mr. White. 私たちの先生は、Mr. White です

3. me, you, him, her, us, them「～に、～を、～と、～が」などの意味。動作や関係の対象となる。
   on, with, before などの前置詞の前は必ずこの形。
   I know her. 私は彼女を知っている

4. mine, yours, hers, his, ours, theirs 「～のもの」という意味。属する人やモノも含む。
   This is hers. これは彼女のものだ

▶Practice 8 Pronouns 代名詞

Put the correct pronouns from Grammar 1 on page 9 and Grammar 4 on page 14 in the spaces below.

P. 9 の 1 と P.14 の Grammar 4 を参考にして、空欄に正しい代名詞を入れましょう。* this/that は使えません。

__________ name is Rika. __________ am 20 years old. There are four people in __________ family. __________ have one brother. __________ name is Ken. __________ is in high school. He often helps me with __________ homework, so I really like him. __________ family lives in Kyoto. __________ is a beautiful city. Kyoto is famous for __________ history. __________ study Chinese at university. __________ is a difficult language. __________ best friend is from China. __________ name is Mei. __________ parents live in Beijing. __________ misses __________ parents, so she wants to visit __________ in China soon.

▶Practice 9 My Introduction 私の自己紹介

Fill in the sentences below to make true sentences about yourself. Look at Practice 7 to help you.

自分についての自己紹介を以下の空欄を埋めて完成させましょう。Practice 7 の自己紹介文を参考にしてください。

Hello, everybody. My name is ________________. I'm a student. I study ________________. I want to be a ________________ in the future. I'm ________________ years old. I live in ________________. In my free time, I like to ________________. There are __________ people in my family.

After you have finished, read your introduction to the class. Try to look at the class while you speak.

空欄を埋めたらクラスメイトに自己紹介文を読んでください。丸暗記する必要はありませんが、ときどきクラスメイトの顔を見ながら読んでみましょう。

Grammar 5

10

Yes/No questions with "be" and "do"

be 動詞と一般動詞 do を使った Yes/No 質問文

Questions and answers with "be" **be 動詞を使った質問文と答え**

Are you a university student? Yes, I ***am***.

Is he a freshman? No, he ***isn't***. ***He's*** a sophomore.

Are we in the same class? Yes, we ***are***.

Questions and answers with "do" **do を使った質問文と答え**

Do you study business? No, I ***don't***. I study engineering*.

Does she live in Tokyo? Yes, she ***does***.

Do you want to be a teacher? Yes, I ***do***. I want to work in a kindergarten*.

Do we have a lot of homework? Yes, we ***do***.

* engineering エンジニアリング kindergarten 幼稚園

▶Practice 10 Matching 質問に合った答えをさがそう

Put the correct letters for the answers in the space.

1～8までの質問に対する最も適切な答えを A から H の中から選びましょう。

____ 1. Are you a freshman?	A. No, I don't. I study computer science.
____ 2. Do you study nursing?	B. That's a good idea. Let's get some coffee.
____ 3. Is English difficult?	C. No, they're from Australia.
____ 4. Are they American?	D. Yes, it is. Grammar is hard for me.
____ 5. Do you live in Osaka?	E. Yes, I am. I go to City University.
____ 6. Are you a university student?	F. No, I don't. I live in Kobe.
____ 7. Do you have many classes?	G. No, I'm not. I'm a sophomore.
____ 8. Do you want to take a break?	H. Not so many. I have 12 a week.

▶Practice 11 Find Someone Who ... こんな人を探そう

First, complete the questions on the left of the chart below. Then find someone who answers "yes" to the questions and write their names on the right. Try to talk to as many people as you can.

表の左側の質問文を完成させ、その質問に Yes と答えられる人（否定の質問で聞かれたら答えは No）を見つけたら、右側の欄に記入してください。できるだけ多くの人に質問しましょう。

Example: Question: Do you sleep eight hours a night?
Answer: Yes, I do. (Write down the person's name)

Find Someone Who ... こんな人を見つけましょう	**Name** 名前
1. ... sleeps eight hours a night. Question: ***Do you sleep eight hours a night*** ?	
2. ... plays computer games. Question: ____________________?	
3. ... is good at sports. Question: ____________________?	
4. ... wants to travel overseas.* Question: ____________________?	
5. ... is a freshman* or a sophomore.* Question: ____________________?	
6. ... likes to cook. Question: ____________________?	
7. ... has a part-time job. Question: ____________________?	
8. ... is from a big city. Question: ____________________?	

* overseas 海外に、海外の　freshman 大学1年生　sophomore 大学2年生

▶Practice 12 Find the Mistakes 間違い探し

Look at the sentences below. Each one has a mistake. Find the mistakes and then write the correct sentences. Sometimes you have a choice about how to correct the sentences.

以下の１～８までの文章にはそれぞれ間違いがあります。間違いを見つけて正しい文に書き換えましょう。

1. What do she do?

____

2. We are America.

____

3. Where is Pedro come from?

____

4. I live by yourself.

____

5. I live Yokohama.

____

6. I'm 19 year old.

____

7. In my free time, I like play the piano.

____

8. Kyoto are a beautiful city.

____

Unit 2

What Do You Do?

あなたの職業は？

Speaking スピーキング

Practice the following dialogues with a partner. After you have practiced the model conversation a few times, substitute the underlined information with the words in the boxes.

以下の会話をパートナーと練習してください。数回練習したら、下線の部分を枠内の表現に言いかえて再度練習しください。

Dialogue 1 会話 1 11

Mari: What do you do, Dan?

Dan: I'm a university student. I study business.*(1) What about you, Mari?

Mari: I go to university, too. I study nursing.*(2)

Dan: Oh, really? Nursing*(2) sounds interesting.

1. psychology* history*	2. dentistry* biology*

Dialogue 2 会話 2 12

David: What do you do, Peggy?

Peggy: I'm a teacher. I teach English at a university.

David: Great! Where do your students come from?(1)

Peggy: Many different countries.(2)

David: Do you like your job?

Peggy: Yes, I do. It's interesting and I really like my students.

1. are your students from?	2. All over the world

* business ビジネス nursing 看護 psychology 心理学 history 歴史 dentistry 歯学 biology 生物学

Grammar 1

The difference between "What do you do?" and "What are you doing?"

動詞の現在形と進行形の違い

"What do you do?" is asking about a person's job. "What are you doing?" (present continuous tense) is asking what the person is doing "right now."

"What do you do?" は " 仕事 " について聞く質問です。一方で "What are you doing?" は、相手が " 今この瞬間 " 何をしているのか、を聞く質問です。

Grammar 2

13

Present Simple Tense (with "wh" questions and answers)

一般動詞現在形（"Wh" 質問とその答え）

What do you do?	I'm a university student.
What university do you go to?	(I go to) City University.
What do you study?	(I study) Economics.
Where do you live?	(I live in) Fukuoka.
What do you (like to) do in your free time?	I like to read.
What do you want to do in the future?	I want to travel to many countries.

►Practice 1 Questions and Answers (1) 自分のことについて答えよう（1）

Write complete questions using the words below. Number 4 has been done for you.

文頭にある単語の順序を変えて正しい質問文を完成させましょう。4. の答えは例として参考にしてください。

1. What / name: ____________________________?
2. How old: ____________________________?
3. What / do: ____________________________?
4. What / university / go: *What university do you go to*?
5. What / study: ____________________________?
6. Where / live: ____________________________?
7. What / free time: ____________________________?
8. What / want to do / the future: ____________________________?

▶Practice 2 Questions and Answers (2) 質問と答え(2)

Write answers to the questions in **Practice 1** (1 to 8) that are true for you. Write in complete sentences.

Practice 1 (1 ～ 8) の質問に対する自分の答えを書きましょう。完全な文で答えてください。

Example (for question number 1): My name is Mie Kobayashi.

1. ____________________
2. ____________________
3. ____________________
4. ____________________
5. ____________________
6. ____________________
7. ____________________
8. ____________________

▶Practice 3 Pair Work ペアワーク

Ask your partner the questions in **Practice 1** and write their answers below. Be sure to write in full sentences.

パートナーに Practice 1 の質問をして答えを枠内に書きましょう。完全な文で書いてください。

1. ____________________
2. ____________________
3. ____________________
4. ____________________
5. ____________________
6. ____________________
7. ____________________
8. ____________________

▶Practice 4 Interview インタビュー

You will do a survey. First, write the questions. When finished, ask your questions to different students. Write their name and notes for each answer.

クラスメートにインタビューをしてみましょう。まず質問文を作り、そのあと色々な人に質問をして、その答えを書き入れましょう。答えてくれた人の名前を入れるのを忘れずに。質問文は、“You/your ～”を主語にして聞き、答えは、“He/She”または“Her～/His～”を主語にしてください。

Example:	What/name? Question: What's your name ____?	Name: Mariko Ono Answer: Mariko Ono

	Questions	**Names and Answers**
1.	What / name? Question: ____________?	Name: Answer:
2.	How old ...? Question: ____________?	Name: Answer:
3.	What / do? Question: ____________?	Name: Answer:
4.	What university / go to? Question: ____________?	Name: Answer:
5.	What / study? Question: ____________?	Name: Answer:
6.	Where / live? Question: ____________?	Name: Answer:
7.	What / free time? Question: ____________?	Name: Answer:
8.	What / want to do in the future? Question: ____________?	Name: Answer:

Now, write the answers you got to your questions. Use full sentences.

枠内の質問に対する答えを完全な文で書きましょう。

Example (for question number 1): His name is Yoshiyuki Igarashi.

1. ____
2. ____
3. ____
4. ____
5. ____

6. ______________________________

7. ______________________________

8. ______________________________

▶Practice 5 Vocabulary 単語表現 14

Choose the correct word from the box for each picture.

絵の職業を表す最も適切な単語を枠内から選びましょう

Example:

doctor

professor dentist firefighter* ~~doctor~~
chefs police officers pilot cashier*
nurse servers* businessperson

1. ____________

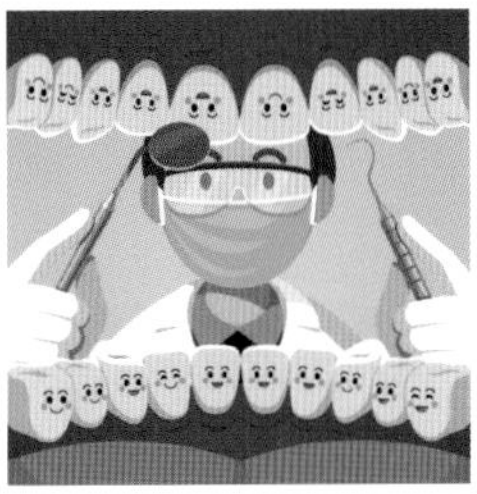

2. ____________

3. ____________

4. ____________

5. ____________

6. ____________

7. ____________

8. ____________

9. ____________

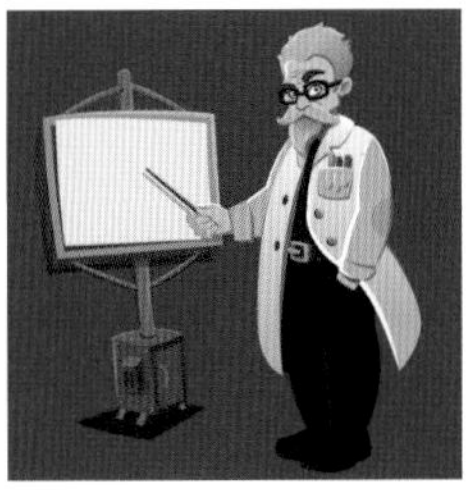

10. ____________

* firefighter 消防士 cashier レジ係 server 給仕人、接客係

▶Practice 6 Matching 職業を説明しよう

Put the correct letter in each space to make a sentence.

1～12の職業を説明するものを、A～Lの中から選びましょう。

1. A professor ______
2. A police officer ______
3. A doctor ______
4. A businessperson ______
5. A taxi driver ______
6. A salesperson ______
7. A banker ______
8. A pilot ______
9. A firefighter ______
10. A chef ______
11. A dentist ______
12. An actor ______

A. makes food in a restaurant.
B. helps people who are sick.
C. sells* things for a company or a shop.
D. is in movies or TV dramas.
E. teaches students at a university.
F. flies airplanes.
G. drives people to different places.
H. stops crime*.
I. works with money.
J. works in an office.
K. puts out* fires.
L. takes care of* your teeth.

* sell 売る　crime 犯罪　put out 消す　take care of 手入れをする

▶Practice 7 Listening: What Does She or He Do? リスニング：彼女／彼の職業は？ 15

Listen and guess what job the speaker does. Choose the job from the box and write sentences like the example below.

英文を聞いてその人の職業を枠内から選び、例を参考にして文を書きましょう。

doctor	actor	pilot	firefighter	professor
university student	chef	businessperson	~~nurse~~	

Example: You hear: "I work in a large hospital. I take care of* patients* and give them medicine.*"
You write: She's a nurse.

1. ______________________.
2. ______________________.
3. ______________________.
4. ______________________.
5. ______________________.
6. ______________________.
7. ______________________.
8. ______________________.

* take care of 世話をする　patient 患者　medicine 薬　famous 有名な　dangerous 危険な　be 動詞+ on fire 火事になる　put the fire out 火を消す　customer 客　injury/injuries ケガ　manage 管理する　nursing 看護　take classes 授業をとる

▶Practice 8 Gesture Game: What's My Job? ジェスチャーゲーム：私の職業は？

Your teacher will give you a job title. Act out the job without speaking. Try to get your group to guess what your job is.

先生から示された職業を、口頭ではなくジェスチャーでグループのメンバーに説明してみましょう。

Key Example: Are you a / an (teacher)?
Yes, I am. / No, I'm not.
I give up!

▶Practice 9 Group Work: What's My Job? グループワーク：私の職業は？ 16

One person in your group will think of a job. The other members ask questions to try to find out what the job is. The questions should all be "Yes / No" questions.

グループ内で一人が仕事を一つ選びます。他のメンバーは、"Yes/No" で答えられる質問をして、その仕事が何かをあててください。

Example:
A: Do you work inside?
B: Sometimes.
C: OK. Do you work 9 to 5?
B: No.
D: Do you work at night?
B: Sometimes.
E: Do you work at home?
B: No.
C: Do you sell something?
B: No.
F: Do you drive a car?
B: Sometimes.
A: Do you wear a uniform?
B: Yes.
D: Are you a police officer?
B: No.

Now it is your turn to play "What's my job?" But first, you need to prepare some questions. Work with a group and add questions to the chart below.

以下の表にいくつか質問があります。グループ内で話し合いながら、新しい質問を作り、表に加えてください。

Do you ...	Do you work ...	Do you use ...	Do you wear ...	Is your job ...
sell something? *drive a car?*	*inside?* *9 to 5?* *at night?* *at home?*	*your hands?* *a computer?*	*a uniform?*	*dangerous?*

▶Practice 10 Bingo ビンゴゲーム 17

Write all of the job names from the box below in the bingo card, one job name per box.

枠内の単語を順不同でビンゴカードに記入しましょう。ひとつのボックスにひとつの単語を書き入れて 下さい。

professor	dentist	firefighter	chef	caregiver	police officer
pilot	cashier	nurse	server	doctor	businessperson
taxi driver	salesperson	banker	actor		

Now listen to your teacher describe different jobs. You must listen carefully because you won't hear the actual words, but hints that help you guess the words. Cross off the words corresponding to the hints. When you have crossed off four words in a row on your card, shout "Bingo!"

先生が様々な職業について説明します。ヒントをよく聞いて，当てはまる単語があれは消していきます。縦か横一列に 4 つ消すことができたら、大きな声で "Bingo!" と言いましょう。

Bingo Card

Unit 3
I'm Busy!
忙しい！

Grammar 1
Adverbs of Frequency
頻度を表す副詞

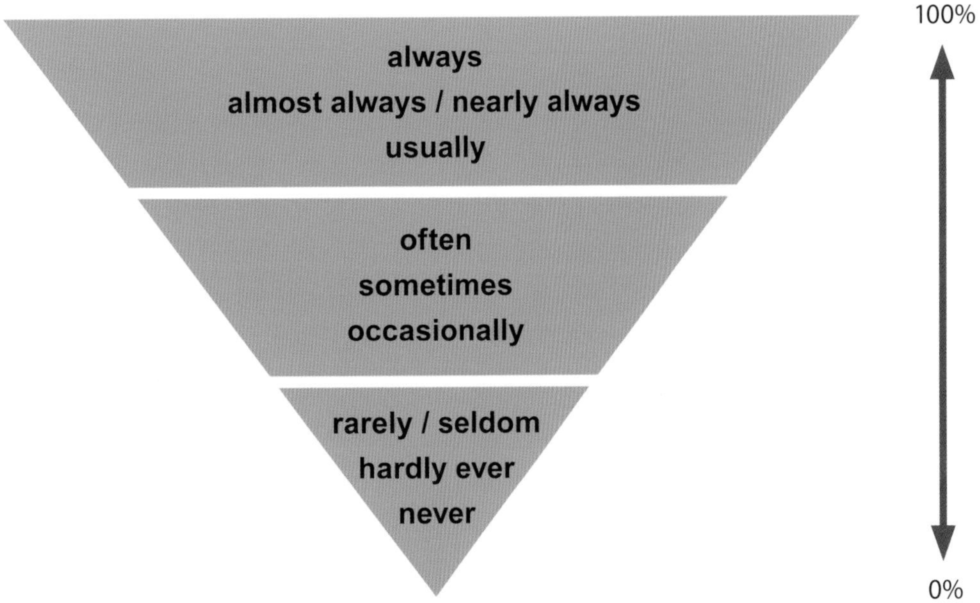

▶**Practice 1 Adverbs of Frequency** 頻度を表す副詞
Study Grammar 1 and try to remember the "Adverbs of Frequency." Then turn to **Appendix 1** and do the exercise.
Grammar 1 の " 頻度を表す副詞 " を勉強したら、Appendix 1 を開いて練習問題をやってみましょう。

Speaking スピーキング

Practice the following dialogues with a partner. After you have practiced the model conversation a few times, substitute the underlined information with the words in the boxes.

以下の会話をパートナーと練習してください。数回練習したら、下線の部分を枠内の表現に言いかえて再度練習しください。

Dialogue 1 会話 1 18

Haruka: How are you doing*, Brad?

Brad: I'm busy! On weekdays*, I always (1) study at the university. I'm often there from 9 a.m. to 6 p.m.

Haruka: How about on weekends*?

Brad: Well, I usually (2) play soccer and I occasionally* play tennis.

Haruka: Good for you*!

Brad: How about you, Haruka? Do you play any sports?

Haruka: No, I'm lazy*. I rarely (3) exercise.

1. almost always nearly always	2. often* sometimes	3. seldom* hardly ever*

* How are you doing? 元気？（最近どう？） weekdays 平日 weekends 週末
occasionally ときどき Good for you! いいね！えらいね！ lazy なまけた
often 頻繁に seldom めったに〜ない hardly ever めったに〜ない

Dialogue 2 会話 2 19

Brad: Do you have a part-time job?

Haruka: Yes, I do. I work in a bakery.

Brad: How often?

Haruka: Once a week. (1) How about you, Brad? Do you have a part-time job?

Brad: Yes, I teach English in a cram school* every other day.* (2)

Haruka: Wow, you sound* busy.

1. twice a week three times a week	2. once or twice a week two or three times a week

* cram school 塾 every other day 一日おきに sound〜 〜のようだ、〜らしい

Grammar 2

How Often?

どのくらい頻度で？

How often do you watch a movie?	Once a week.
How often do you brush your teeth?	Three times a day.
How often do you go on a trip?	Once or twice a year.
How often do you go shopping?	Every other day.

Every day (week / month / year)	毎日
Once a day (week / month / year)	1日1回（週／月／年）
Twice a day (week / month / year)	1日2回（週／月／年）
Three times a day (week / month / year)	1日3回（週／月／年）
Every other day (week / month / year)	日おきに（週／月／年）

▶Practice 2　Matching　質問に合った答えを探そう

Match the questions on the left with the answers on the right. Put the correct letters on the lines.

1～5までの質問に対する最も適切な答えをAからEの中から選びましょう。

____ 1. How often do you eat sushi?	A. I go five days a week.
____ 2. How often do you play tennis?	B. Three times a week. I work at a café.
____ 3. How often do you work?	C. Three times a day, after I eat.
____ 4. How often do you go to university?	D. I play once a week.
____ 5. How often do you brush your teeth?	E. Never. I don't like fish.

▶Practice 3　Writing (1): How Often?　ライティング(1)：どのくらい頻繁に？

How often do you do the following activities? Look at the pictures. Write a "How often do you...?" question. Then write answers that are true for you. Refer to the frequency expressions on page 27. Write in full sentences.

頻度の表現を参考にして、絵を見ながら自分のこととして質問に答えてみましょう。完全な文を書いてください。

Example: How ***often*** do you drive?
Answer: I ***often*** drive. (or) I drive ***every day***.

1. How often do you play computer games?

Answer: ______________________________

2. How often do you go to an amusement park*?

Answer: ______________________________

3. How often do you eat rice?

Answer: ______________________________

4. How often do you visit a shrine*?

Answer: ______________________________

5. How often do you buy clothes?

Answer: ______________________________

6. How often do you use your smartphone?

Answer: ______________________________

* amusement park 遊園地　shrine 神社

7. How often do you listen to music?

Answer: ______________________________

8. How often do you ride a train?

Answer: ______________________________

9. How often do you go to a coffee shop?

Answer: ______________________________

10. How often do you sleep in class?

Answer: ______________________________

Grammar 3

21

How Long?*

どのくらいの時間／期間

How long does it take you to brush your teeth?	About three minutes.
How long do you study every day?	About one or two hours.
How long do you work usually?	About four hours.
How long is your summer vacation?	Six weeks.

* How long どのくらいの時間

▶Practice 4 Writing (2): How long? ライティング(2):どのくらいの時間？

Write answers that are true for you.

自分のこととして質問に答えましょう。

Example: A: How long do you usually watch TV every day?
B: It depends.* I sometimes watch for* two or three hours.

1. A: How long do you spend* in the shower/bath?

   B: ____

2. A: How long do you study every day?

   B: ____

3. A: How long do you spend online every day?

   B: ____

4. A: How long does it take you to get to school / university?

   B: ____

5. A: How long does it take you to eat lunch?

   B: ____

6. A: How long is your English class?

   B: ______________________________

▶Practice 5 Listening リスニング 22

Listen to a university student talk about what he usually does on Friday. Write in the missing words.

ある大学生が彼の一日について話しています。空欄を埋めましょう。

Today ____________. I almost always ____________ on Friday and ____________ go out* with my friends. We ____________ karaoke because we all ____________. However, we're ____________ to karaoke today. We often ____________ together at a cheap* restaurant, because we ____________ money. It's now 5 p.m. My last ____________ finished. I'm now ____________ so I'm walking ____________ station. I'm tired today and I have a lot of ____________. I hope ____________ I can go out together next weekend.

* go out 出かける　cheap 安い

Grammar 4 23

Time Expressions

時間を表す

I get up ***at**** 6:15 ***in*** the morning.

I eat lunch ***from*** 12:15 ***to**** 1:15 ***in*** the afternoon.

I arrive* home ***at*** 8:00 ***in**** the evening.

I go to bed* ***at*** 11 p.m. ***at**** night.

I study ***until**** 1:00 a.m. ***on*** Friday so I go to bed ***late***.*

I wake up ***early**** ***on*** weekdays.

I wake up ***late on*** weekends.

I sleep ***until*** noon* ***on**** Sunday.

* at ～ = ～時に　from ～ to ～ = ～時から～時まで　arrive 着く
in the + morning, afternoon, evening 朝、午後、夕方に　go to bed 寝る
at+night 夜に　until ～まで　late 遅く　early 早く　noon 正午に
on ～ = ～曜日に、～日に、(週末 weekends/ 平日 weekdays) に

▶Practice 6 Time Expressions (1) 時間を表す (1)

Put the words from the box below into the correct spaces.

枠内から適切な前置詞を選び、空欄を埋めましょう。カッコ内の数字はその前置詞が何度使えるかを示しています。

from　to　at　on　in (3 times)

I'm a nurse. I work at a hospital. I often work _________ night. I usually work _________ 11 p.m. _________ 7 a.m. I also sometimes work _________ weekends. It's difficult to meet my friends, because they work _________ the morning and _________ the afternoon. That's why I sometimes meet them _________ the evening.

in　from　to　at　on　late　until (2 times)　early

I'm a businessperson. I usually wake up _________, around 6 a.m. _________ the morning. I arrive* at my office _________ 8:30 a.m. every day _________ Monday _________ Friday. I often work _________ , sometimes _________ 10 p.m. I'm often tired, so I sleep _________ 10 a.m. _________ Saturday and Sunday mornings.

* arrive 着く

Culture Note

Time Expressions

時間を表す

- When talking about time, we use "a.m." and "p.m." or "in the morning" and "in the afternoon." "We don't use times like 14:00, like many Japanese do. Therefore, we say 2 p.m., not 14:00.
  午前、午後を明確にしたいときは、a.m. / p.m.、または in the morning (午前) / in the afternoon (午後) という表現を使い、14:00 や 21:00 という言い方はしません。時間を表すときは、数字だけでもオーケーです。2 時と言いたいときは、Two あるいは "2"
- "O'clock" is only used one time per hour. We can say "2 o'clock", but not "2:30 o'clock."
  "o'clock" は、一時間ごとのきっかりした時間にしか使えないので、2:30 は 2:30 o'clock とは言えません。また、"o'clock" はたいてい省略されます。
- We often use "around" and "about" for time. 2 時頃と言いたいときは around 2、about 2 となります。
- "Noon" is used for 12:00 in the day. "Midnight" is used for 12:00 at night.
  "Noon" は 12 時を、"Midnight" は夜中の 12 時を意味します。

▶Practice 7 Koji's Day Kojiの一日

Koji is a university student in Tokyo. **Student A:** Look at Koji's schedule below. **Student B:** Look at Koji's schedule in **Appendix 2.** Work in pairs and ask and answer questions to find the missing information.

Koji は東京の大学生です。Student A は下の Koji のスケジュールを見て、Student B は Appendix 2 のスケジュールを見てください。お互いに質問し合って空欄を埋めましょう。

Examples:

Question: What does Koji do at 6 a.m.? Answer: He wakes up (at 6 a.m.).
Question: What time does Koji wake up? Answer: (He wakes up) At 6.a.m.
Question: What does Koji do from 7:30 to 8:40 a.m.? Answer: He rides the train.

Student A

Time	Activity
6 a.m.	Koji wakes up.
6:15 a.m.	Koji eats breakfast.
7 a.m.	
7:30 a.m. – 8:40 a.m.	Koji rides the train.
	Koji arrives* at the university.
8:55 a.m.	Koji enters the classroom.
9 a.m. – 10:30 a.m.	
10:30 a.m. – 10:45 a.m.	Koji drinks a cup of coffee.
	Koji has his second class.
12:15 p.m. – 1 p.m.	Koji eats lunch.
1 p.m. – 2:30 p.m.	
2:30 p.m. – 3:30 p.m.	Koji talks with his friends.
	Koji studies in the library.
6 p.m.	Koji leaves* the university.
6 p.m. – 6:10 p.m.	
6:10 p.m. – 7:20 p.m.	Koji goes home by train.
	Koji buys food at the supermarket.
8 p.m.	Koji arrives home and cooks dinner.
9 p.m.	
10:30 p.m.	Koji takes a shower*.
	Koji goes to bed.

* arrive 着く　leave 出る、去る　take a shower シャワーをあびる

▶Practice 8 Matching 質問に合った答えを探そう

Put the correct letters for the answers in the space.

1 ～ 7 までの質問に対する最も適切な答えを A ～ G の中から選びましょう。

___ 1. How often do you watch TV?	A. Around 12 midnight on weekdays.
___ 2. When do you study?	B. Every day.
___ 3. How long is the class?	C. Yes. I usually sleep until 9 or 10 a.m.
___ 4. How long do you usually sleep?	D. It's 90 minutes.
___ 5. What time is it?	E. About six or seven hours a night.
___ 6. When do you usually go to bed?	F. After my last class. I do my homework in the library.
___ 7. Do you get up late on Sundays?	G. It's now 3:15.

▶Practice 9 Time Expressions (2) 時間を表す (2)

Answer the following questions. For number 4 and number 5, find the mistake and write the correct answer.

以下の質問に答えましょう。4. と 5. は、間違いを直して正しい答えを書きましょう。

1. What time is it?

____

2. What time is it?

____

3. What's another way to say "about" in "Let's meet *about* 6 p.m."?

____

4. Find and correct the mistake: "I have class from 14:45 to 15:45."

____

5. Find and correct the mistake: "I go to bed at 11:30 o'clock."

____

►Practice 10 Time Expressions (3) 時間を表す (3)

Answer the following questions. Use full sentences.

以下の質問に答えましょう。例を参考に完全な文章で答えてください。

Example: What time do you go to bed on weeknights?
I usually go to bed around 11 p.m.

1. What time do you wake up on school days?

2. What time do you wake up on Sundays?

3. Do you usually go to sleep before 12 midnight?

4. When do you usually watch TV?

5. What time is your first class on Monday morning?

6. What time do you usually eat lunch?

Pair Work ペアワーク

Now take turns asking and answering the above questions with a partner.

ペアワーク：今度はパートナーに上の質問をして答えてもらいましょう。

▶Practice 11 Survey インタビュー

First, complete the questions below. Then ask the questions to different students in the class. Write down their names and answers in full sentences.

まず最初に 1 ～ 6 の質問を完成させましょう。それぞれ別のクラスメイトに質問し、右枠にその人の答えを完全な文（例を参照）と名前を書いてください。

Examples:

Emi: How often do you watch TV?
Rei: I watch TV every day.
Emi: OK. And what's your name?
Rei: It's Rei.
Emi: Thank you, Rei.

Name: ***Rei.***
Answer: ***Rei watches TV every day.***

	Questions	Names and Answers
1.	How often ... watch TV?	Name: Answer:
2.	What ... usually watch on TV?	Name: Answer:
3.	When ... watch TV?	Name: Answer:
4.	What ... favorite TV program?	Name: Answer:
5.	Who ... favorite actor?	Name: Answer:
6.	What ... like more, TV or YouTube?	Name: Answer:

Review Units 1 - 3

Unit 1 から Unit 3 までの復習

▶Practice 1 Information Exchange 情報交換

Student A: Look at the information below. **Student B**: Turn to **Appendix 3**. **Student A**: Ask and answer questions as in the Examples to fill in the missing information for numbers 1 and 3.

Student A は以下の画像を見て、Student B は Appendix 3 を見て下さい。Student A は 1 と 3 について Student B に質問し、答えを空欄に記入しましょう。

Examples:

What's his/her name?
How old is she/he?
What does she/he do?
Where does she/he live?
What does she/he do in her/his free time?

How do you spell that?
Pardon?

Student A

1.

Name: ______________
Age: ______________
Job: ______________
Where / live: ______________
Free time: ______________

2.

Name: Yuji Suzuki
Age: 58
Job: Banker
Where / live: Yokohama
Free time: Plays golf

3.

Name: ______________
Age: ______________
Job: ______________
Where / live: ______________
Free time: ______________

4.

Name: Zubby Ibrahim
Age: 32
Job: Doctor
Where / live: Lagos
Free time: Plays soccer

Review Units 1 - 3

▶Practice 2 **Board Game** ボードゲーム

To play the board game below, you will need to make groups. Follow the instructions.
以下のルールに従って、グループでボードゲームをしてみましょう。

1. Use small pieces of paper with your initials on them as markers.
   小さな紙に自分のイニシャルを書き，自分の駒にします。
2. Toss a coin or play 'rock, paper, scissors' to decide who goes first.
   コインを使って (またはジャンケンで) 誰から始めるかを決めます。

START HERE

1. What's your name?

2. Are you a university student?

3. Are you a junior?

4. What do you study?

5. Where do you live?

6. What do you like to do in your free time?

7. What do you want to do in the future?

8. How old are you?

9. Is English difficult?

10. Do you have many classes?

11. Are you American?

12. What do you do?

13. Do you want to travel overseas?

14. Do you have a part-time job?

15. Do you play any sports?

● ● ●

3. Each player then takes turns by tossing a coin. If the coin lands face up, move two spaces. If the coin lands face down, move one space.
順番にコインを投げ、表が出たら 2 マス、裏か出たら 1 マス進みます。
4. When you land on a space, answer the question. Answer any follow-up questions.
止まったマスの質問に答え，追加の質問にも答えます。

Useful expressions: 便利な表現：

I'll go first. 私から先にします。　Is it my turn? 私の番ですか？　It's your turn. あなたの番です。

22.
How long do you spend eating breakfast?

23.
What time do you usually wake up?

24.
What do you usually do on Sundays?

GOAL!

21.
Who's your favorite actor?

20.
How often do you sleep in class?

19.
How often do you go shopping?

16.
How often do you ride a train?

17.
How often do you go on a trip?

18.
How often do you look at your smartphone?

Unit 4

What Does She Look Like?

彼女の外見はどんな？

Speaking スピーキング

Practice the following dialogues with a partner. After you have practiced the model conversation a few times, substitute the underlined information with the words in the boxes.

以下の会話をパートナーと練習してください。数回練習したら、下線の部分を枠内の表現に言いかえて再度練習しください。

Dialogue 1 24

Carla: Tell me about your sister. How old is she?

Mai: She's 17 years old, so she's younger(1) than me.

Carla: Is she a high-school student?

Mai: Yes, she is.

Carla: What does she look like?

Mai: Well, she's short(2) and has long(3) black(4) hair. I think she's cute.

1. older	2. tall medium* height*	3. short medium-length*	4. brown blond

Dialogue 2 25

Reina: Do you have a boyfriend, Shawna?

Shawna: No, but I really like John. He's the new guy in my class.

Reina: Oh, yeah? What does he look like?

Shawna: He has a beard* and a mustache*. Here's a picture of him.

Reina: Wow! He's handsome(1)!

Shawna: I think so, too. He plays basketball, so he's very tall.(2)

1. good looking*	2. muscular*

*medium 中くらいの　height 高さ　medium-length 中くらいの長さ　beard 口ひげ（あごの周り）
mustache 口ひげ（鼻の下）　good looking ルックスのよい　muscular 筋肉たくましい

Grammar 1

26

Describing People

人について説明する

Subject + be verb + adjective
主語＋ be 動詞＋形容詞

He ***is*** good looking.
She ***is*** pretty.
They ***are*** young.
Her hair ***is*** long.

Subject + have/has + noun
主語＋ have/has ＋名詞

He ***has*** a mustache.
She ***has*** short brown hair.
They ***have*** black hair.
She ***has*** long hair.

Key Words: Describing People キーワード：人について説明する 27

1. Age: How old is he?

He's young. He's a teenager. He's middle-aged. He's old/elderly.*

She's in her early teens.* She's in her mid-thirties.* She's in her late fifties.*

*elderly 年配の　teens 13 才から 19 才の若者たち　mid-thirties 30 代半ば　late fifties 50 代後半

2. Height: How tall is he?

He's tall. She's short.

How tall are they?

They're average* height.

* average 平均的な

3. Hair: What color is her hair?

She has black hair.

She has blond hair.

She has red hair.

She has gray hair.

How long is her hair?

She has short hair.

She has medium-length* hair.

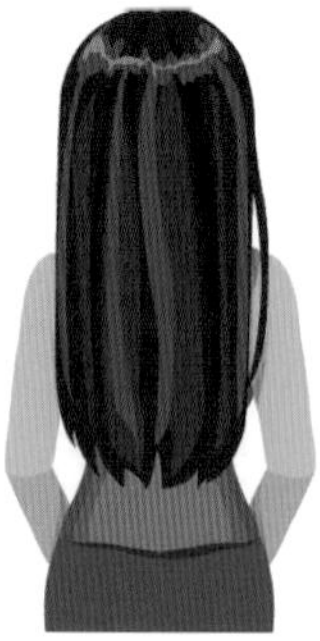

She has long hair.

*straight まっすぐな wavy ウェーブのかかった medium-length セミロングの

4. Eyes: What color are her eyes?

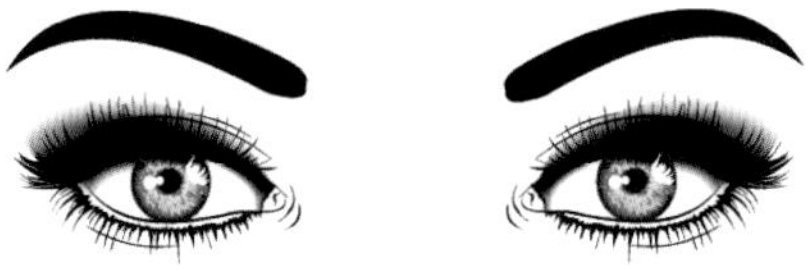

She has blue eyes.

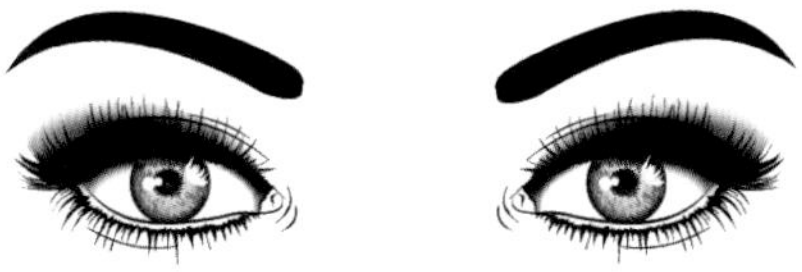

She has green eyes.

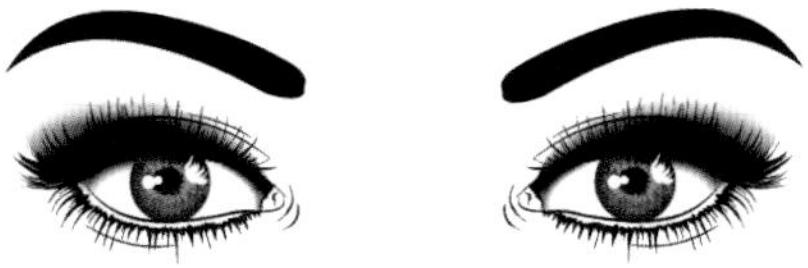

She has brown eyes.

5. What does he / she look like?

She wears glasses.

She has long black hair.

She has wavy red hair.

She has straight blond hair.

She has medium-length gray hair.

He's handsome / good looking.

She's beautiful / good looking.

She's pretty / cute.

He has a beard and a mustache.*

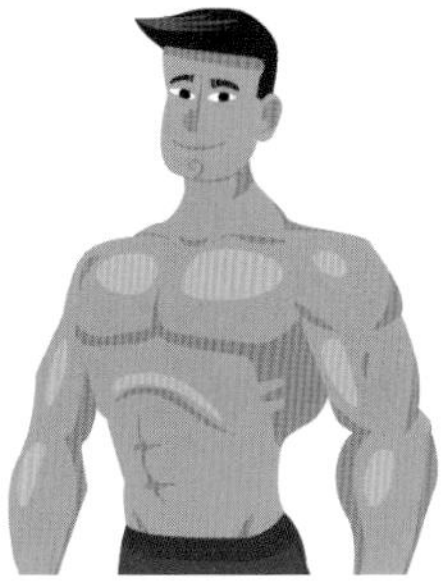

He's strong and muscular.*

* mustache 鼻の下の口ひげ　muscular 筋肉質の

▶Practice 1 Faces 顔

Example: Who has wavy hair?
May and Jalaya have wavy hair.

1. Who has long black hair? (Two people)

____

2. Who has green eyes?

____

3. Who has blue eyes? (Two people)

____

4. Who has brown hair? (Two people)

____

5. Who has straight blond hair?

____

6. Who has red hair with bangs*?

____

* bangs 前髪

▶Practice 2 Verbs 動詞

Put the correct verb ("be" or "have") with the correct verb form in the sentences below.

空欄に be 動詞か have/has を適切な形にして入れましょう。

1. He ________________ tall.
2. She ________________ long black hair.
3. The children ________________ cute.
4. My teacher ________________ a beard.
5. My hair ________________ brown.
6. I ________________ green eyes.
7. I ________________ long brown hair.

▶Practice 3 Matching 質問に合った答えをさがそう

Put the correct letters for the answers in the space.

1 ～ 10 までの質問に対する最も適切な答えを A ～ J の中から選びましょう。

_____ 1. Is she pretty?

_____ 2. How old is your brother?

_____ 3. How old are they?

_____ 4. Does he wear contact lenses?

_____ 5. How tall is he?

_____ 6. What does he look like?

_____ 7. Is his hair brown?

_____ 8. How long is her hair?

_____ 9. Is he tall?

_____ 10. Does she have bangs?

A. No, it's black.

B. They're both* elderly. They're in their 80's.

C. Yes, she does.

D. Yes, she is. I love her smile.

E. He's tall with brown hair.

F. No, he wears glasses*.

G. No, he's short.

H. He's about 176 centimeters* tall.

I. It's medium-length.

J. He's 15 years old.

* both 両方とも　wear glasses 眼鏡をかける　centimeters センチメートル

▶Practice 4 Memory Game メモリーゲーム

You are now going to play a memory game using cards. Your teacher will tell you what to do. Have fun!

カードを使ってメモリーゲームをしましょう。先生がルールを説明してくれます。Have fun!

Grammar 2

Comparatives

比較級

形容詞を使って比較する

〜より〜だ　主語＋動詞＋形容詞の比較級＋ than ＋名詞

- Comparative adjectives are used to compare two people or things. When using comparatives, we use "than", as shown below.

  形容詞の比較級は、二つのものや人を比べるのに使います。比較級を使うときは "than" を忘れずに。

  Steven is tall. He's ***taller than*** Kara.

- Adding "er" to adjectives is used to make most comparatives. With adjectives ending with "y", the "y" changes to "-ier" for comparatives.

  通常は、"er" を付けて比較級をつくりますが、"y" で終わっている形容詞で y の前が子音のときは、"y" を〜 ier に変えて比較級をつくります。

  Ami's hair is wavy. It's ***wavier than*** mine.
  This chair is heavy. It's ***heavier than*** that one.

- To make comparatives with longer adjectives, "more" is often added before the adjectives. There are no changes to the adjectives.

  2音節以上の形容詞や3音節以上の長めの形容詞 (beautiful, important など) は、通常 "more" を付けて比較級をつくります。

  Eric is handsome. He's ***more handsome than*** other boys in my class.
  Derek is ***more muscular than*** me.

►Practice 5 Comparatives 比較級

Complete the sentences below with the correct form of adjective. Remember to put "than" after each comparative adjective. The first one has been done for you.

カッコ内の形容詞を適切な比較級に変えて、以下の文章を完成させてください。比較級のあとに "than" を入れるのを忘れずに。

1. Tina is ___*taller*___ (tall) ___*than*___ Vince.
2. This dress is ______________ (pretty) ______________ that one.
3. Gina's hair is ______________ (long) ______________ her sister's hair.
4. I'm ______________ (short) ______________ my friend, Bob.
5. Rina is very intelligent*. She's ____________________ (intelligent) ______________ I am.
6. I have wavy hair. It's ______________ (wavy) ____________________ my mother's hair.
7. Jason is ______________ (strong) ____________ his best friend, Adam.
8. My brother is ______________ (muscular) ______________ me.

* intelligent 知的な

►Practice 6 Listening: Which One Is She? リスニング：誰のこと？ 28

Listen to the descriptions of six people and write the correct numbers (from 1 to 6) in the boxes.

6人の人たちを説明する会話を聞いて、誰のことを説明しているのか1～6の番号を空欄に入れましょう。

Himat Ursala Bridget Drake Amanda Paul

▶Practice 7 Who Are You Talking About? 誰について話してるの？

Student A: Look at **Picture A** below and describe five people. Your partner should try to guess each person you are describing. **Student B** then looks at **Picture B** and describes the people to **Student A**.

Student A は Picture A の人たちについてそれぞれ説明してください。パートナーは誰のことを説明しているのかを当ててください。Student B は、Picture B 見て Student A に質問をしてください。

Picture A

Betsy　Jimmy　Brook　Sam　Cindy

Picture B

Harold　Yumi　Alan

Linda　Shoji　Ronnie　June

Unit 5

People and Places

出身地

Speaking スピーキング

Practice the following dialogues with a partner. After you have practiced the model conversation a few times, substitute the underlined information with the words in the boxes.

以下の会話をパートナーと練習してください。数回練習したら、下線の部分を枠内の表現に言いかえて再度練習しください。

Dialogue 1 29

Ms. Suzue: Where are you from, Tan?

Tan: I'm from Vietnam.

Ms. Suzue: Oh, really? I want to go there someday*. What's your hometown*?

Tan: Hanoi.

Ms. Suzue: Wonderful.(1) What's Hanoi like?

Tan: It's a big(2) city. It's crowded(3) but it's exciting.(4)

1. Great	2. large	3. noisy*	4. interesting

Dialogue 2 30

Serina: Ken, you're from Australia, right?

Ken: Yes, I am. I'm from Sydney.

Serina: Sydney? I went there last year. It's pretty.(1) It has some nice(2) beaches.

Ken: How about you, Serina? Where are you from?

Serina: I come from Okinawa. It has some beautiful(3) beaches, too.

Ken: Great! Do you like swimming or surfing*?

Serina: I swim but I don't surf.

1. so nice	2. lovely	3. wonderful

*someday いつか　hometown 故郷　noisy うるさい　surf サーフィンをする

Grammar 1

31

Questions and Answers in the Present Tense

現在形の質問と答え

Where are you from?	(I'm from) Canada.
What's your hometown?	(It's) Osaka.
What's Tokyo like?	It's exciting.
Do you speak English?	Yes, but just a little.
Are you Japanese?	No, I'm Korean.

I want to speak English well.
I hope to go to Europe someday.

▶Practice 1 Missing Words 穴埋め問題

Read the dialogue below and fill in the missing words from the choices given in the boxes.

次の文の空欄に入る最も適切な単語を、枠内から選びましょう。

Part 1

other good I'm from where that is also a lot of
it's in for chocolate famous for are you from wild animals

Amina: Where ____________________, Sam?

Sam: ____________________ Ghana. Do you know ____________________?

Amina: Sure, ______________ Africa. It's famous ____________________, right?

Sam: Yes, but it has ______________ things, not just chocolate. It's ______________ its beaches, forests, and ______________. There is ______________ gold in Ghana.

Part 2

want to go there come from a small town wonderful No, I don't
where do you come from a beautiful Do you know it

Amina: It sounds ____________________. I ____________________.

Sam: And ____________________, Amina?

Amina: I'm from Japan. I ____________________ called Karuizawa. It's ____________________ resort in Nagano. ____________________?

Sam: ____________________. Sorry.

►Practice 2 Nationality and Language 国籍と言語 32

Student A should look at the chart below. **Student B** should turn to **Appendix 4**. Take turns and ask questions. Write down the answers in the blanks below, as shown in the example.

Student A は下の絵を見て、Student B は Appendix 4 を見てください。交代で質問して、例を参考に空欄を埋めましょう。

Example: Student A: Where is Li from?
Student B: She's from China.
Student A: How do you spell "China"?
Student B: "C-H-I-N-A." What's her nationality*?
Student A: She's Chinese. What language does she speak?
Student B: She speaks Chinese.

* nationality 国籍

Student A

Name	Country	Nationality	Language
1. Li (she)	*China*	*Chinese*	*Chinese*
2. Jules (she)		*French*	
3. Antonio (he)	*Spain*		
4. Kristine (she)	*The Philippines*		*Filipino and English*
5. Trang (he)	*Vietnam*		*Vietnamese*
6. Lucas (he)		*Canadian*	
7. Jack (he)		*American*	
8. Rie (she)	*Japan*	*Japanese*	

▶Practice 3 Matching 質問に合った答えをさがそう

Put the correct letters for the answers in the space.

1～8までの質問に対する最も適切な答えをA～Hの中から選びましょう。

____ 1. What's your nationality?	A. Brazil.
____ 2. What's the main language in Canada?	B. I'm American.
____ 3. Is your family here in Japan?	C. No, I'm Vietnamese.
____ 4. Why did you come to Japan?	D. No, they're in Korea.
____ 5. What do you want to do in the future?	E. Yes, it's a wonderful country.
____ 6. Where are you from?	F. I wanted to study and work here.
____ 7. Do you like living in Japan?	G. It's English, but many people speak French.
____ 8. Excuse me, are you Japanese?	H. I want to travel around the world.

▶Practice 4 Writing ライティング

Look at the example sentences below. Write similar sentences using the cues in parentheses (　　).

例文を参考に、カッコ内の単語を使って文を作りましょう。

Examples:

He is Duc. / His name is Duc.	(Duc)
*He is from Vietnam.**	(Vietnam)
*He speaks Vietnamese.**	(Vietnamese)
He is a factory worker.*	(factory worker)
He likes to write messages to friends in his free time.	(write messages to friends)

* Vietnam ベトナム　　Vietnamese ベトナム語　　factory 工場

1. ______________________________ (Feng)

______________________________ (China)

______________________________ (Chinese)

______________________________ (university student)

______________________________ (watch TV)

2. ________________________ (Hans)

________________________ (Germany)

________________________ (German)

________________________ (engineer*)

________________________ (play soccer)

3. ________________________ (Zara)

________________________ (India)

________________________ (several* languages)

________________________ (businessperson)

________________________ (make accessories*)

* engineer エンジニア several いくつかの accessories アクセサリー

▶Practice 5 Pair Work: Running Dictation ペアワーク：ストーリーゲーム

You are now going to do a running dictation. Listen carefully to your teacher's instructions and have fun in this contest. Number 1 has already been done for you. Good luck.

ストーリーゲームです。先生の説明をよく聞いて、このゲームを楽しみましょう。1. は例文です。

Number:

1. ***Hello, everyone. My name is Ken.***

▶Practice 6　Reading　リーディング　🎧33

Travel

Today, more and more Japanese travel overseas* because they want to see the world. Many of them are young people in their twenties, especially young women. However, fewer* Japanese go overseas to study these days*. In addition*, they often study overseas for just a short time. Why? Most Japanese want to graduate from university in four years and then start work right away*.

The Japanese government* is worried about this trend*. Many Japanese companies want to hire* young people who have studied abroad* and who can speak a foreign language well. Also, many companies want people who like challenges.

* overseas 海外の、に　fewer より少ない　these days 最近　in addition ～に加えて
right away すぐに　government 政府　trend 傾向　hire 雇う　abroad 海外へ

True or False　内容把握

Write "T" for true or "F" for false in each of the sentences below.
内容と一致している場合は "T"、一致していなければ "F" を入れましょう。

_____ 1. More Japanese travel to foreign countries than before.

_____ 2. Japanese young people do not like to travel.

_____ 3. More Japanese young women go overseas than young men.

_____ 4. The most popular overseas study programs for Japanese are short.

_____ 5. Many Japanese do not study abroad because they are worried about graduating from university in four years.

_____ 6. Japanese companies do not want to hire young people who have studied overseas.

▶Practice 7 Pair Work: Ideas About Japanese People ペアワーク：日本人について

Below are images some foreign people may have of Japanese people. In pairs, decide whether these ideas are true or not. Then give a reason why you think that way, as in the example. When you have finished, present your ideas to the class.

以下は、外国人が日本人に対して持っていると思われる印象です。パートナーといっしょに自分たちの考えをシェアし、これらの印象が本当かどうかを話し合ってみましょう。そのあとクラスでシェアした意見を発表してください。

Example:
Idea: Japanese are workaholics*.
Your idea: I don't think this is true, because many Japanese don't like to work so hard.

1. Image: Japan is a man's country. Japanese women follow* them.
   Your idea: ______________________________
   ____

2. Image: Japanese are shy people.
   Your idea: ______________________________
   ____

3. Image: Japanese like to wear kimono.
   Your idea: ______________________________
   ____

4. Image: Most Japanese are good at karate.
   Your idea: ______________________________
   ____

* workaholic ワークホリック（仕事中毒）　follow 従う

▶Practice 8 Listening リスニング 🎧34

Listen to a presentation about Christmas in Japan. Fill in the missing words.

日本の家についての説明を聞いて、空欄を埋めましょう。

Hello, everyone. I will talk about ________________. It is one ________________ holidays in Japan, though it is not a national holiday*. Many families have a Christmas tree ______________. Also, many people ______________ Christmas ______________ and buildings in city centers.

On Christmas Eve or Christmas Day, ______________ couples have a romantic dinner ______________ restaurant. Restaurants ______________, so dinner prices are ______________ usual.

On Christmas Day, ________________ exchange* presents and even get a "visit" from Santa Claus, like in Western countries. But Japanese Christmas ______________ in other ways. For dinner, many families ______________ Kentucky Fried Chicken ______________. Most families also ______________ a "Christmas cake" for dessert. Strawberry shortcake is ____________________ cake.

Christmas is an exciting time ______________________.

Thank you for listening.

* national holiday 祝日　exchange 交換する

▶Practice 9 Presentation: Life in Japan プレゼンテーション：日本での生活

Imagine you are giving a talk to foreigners who know little about Japan. Prepare a short presentation describing some part of Japanese life. Look at Practice 7 as an example. You may choose some of the following topics.

日本のことをあまり知らない外国人に、日本についてのプレゼンテーションを行います。日本の生活について、短いプレゼンテーションを作りましょう。Practice 7 と以下のトピックを参考にしてください。自分でトピックを考えても構いません。

Possible topics:

* A Japanese holiday
* Japanese food (*bento*, *sushi*, a holiday food such as *osechi ryōri*, *kyūshoku*, etc.)
* *Kimono* and/or *yukata*
* A popular sport in Japan (baseball, soccer, *sumo*, etc.)
* A popular type of entertainment (*manga*, video games, popular shopping areas such as Harajuku or Shibuya, cosplay, Japanese animation, etc.)
* A famous place in Japan (Kyoto, Kamakura, etc.)
* Cram schools (*juku*) for children
* Japanese homes

Unit 6

Likes and Dislikes

好きなこと、嫌いなこと

Speaking スピーキング

Practice the following dialogues with a partner. After you have practiced the model conversation a few times, substitute the underlined information with the words in the boxes.

以下の会話をパートナーと練習してください。数回練習したら、下線の部分を枠内の表現に言いかえて再度練習しください。

Dialogue 35

Haruka: What's your favorite food, Kelly?

Kelly: I love(1) cheese. Do you like it, Haruka?

Haruka: Yes, I do. I really like Swiss cheese.

Kelly: Yeah, I do, too.(2) I also like blue cheese.

Haruka: Really? I don't. What about Japanese food? Do you like it?

Kelly: Yes, I do. I like sushi a lot, but I don't like(3) *natto.*

Haruka: Neither do I.*(4) And I don't like spicy* food.

Kelly: Oh, I do. I love Indian curry.

1. I really like	2. So do I.	3. I'm not crazy about*	4. Me neither.*

*neither do/does + 名詞 ～も～でない　spicy 辛い
be 動詞+ crazy about ～が大好き (be 動詞+ not crazy about ～=～をそんなに好きではない)
Me neither 私も～でない

Expressing Likes and Dislikes* (1) 36

好き嫌いを表現する

Likes

I love animation.
I really like cats. / I like cats a lot.
I like Japanese pop music.

K-pop is OK.

I don't like doing exercise very much.
I don't like salty food.
I dislike watching romantic comedies.
I hate tomatoes.

Dislikes

* dislike 嫌い (なこと)

▶Practice 1 Writing: Questions and Answers ライティング：自分について答えよう

Write short answers that are true for you, like the example below.

以下の例を参考にして、自分について答えましょう。

Example:

A: Do you like dogs?

B: Yes, I do. I love them.

Useful Expressions

I love it / them.

I like it / them.

They are / It is OK.

I do not like it / them.

I hate it / them.

1. A: Do you like animation?

   B: ______________________________

2. A: Do you like *natto*?

   B: ______________________________

3. A: Do you like cats?

   B: ______________________________

4. A: Do you like taking tests?

   B: ______________________________

5. A: Do you like playing computer games?

   B: ______________________________

6. A: Do you like romantic comedies*?

B: ____

* romantic comedy ロマンチックコメディ

Expressing Likes and Dislikes (2)

37

好き嫌いを表現する

What kind of* music do you like?	I like Korean pop.
What's your favorite* kind of food?	I like Italian food the most.
Who's your favorite singer?	I don't have a favorite singer.
What kind of movies do you dislike?	I dislike horror* movies.
What do you think of* Indian food?	I love it.
How do you like rap?	I don't really like it.

* what kind of どんな種類の　favorite お気に入りの　horror ホラー
What do you think of ~ ? ～についてどう思う？

▶Practice 2 Entertainment Words 娯楽に関する単語

Complete the chart below with the words in the box. The first word has been done for you.

枠内のそれぞれの単語を、枠内の種類別にを分けましょう。

~~adventure~~ animation badminton baseball basketball classical
comedy documentary drama horror jazz news pop rap
rock science fiction soccer sumo talk show tennis volleyball

TV/Movies	Music	Sports
1. ***adventure***	1.	1.
2.	2.	2.
3.	3.	3.
4.	4.	4.
5.	5.	5.
6.		6.
7.		7.
8.		
9.		

▶Practice 3 Entertainment* Survey (1) 娯楽についてのインタビュー（1） 38

First, write answers to the questions under "You." Use some of the words in Practice 2 to help you. When you are finished, ask the questions to a partner and write his or her answers under "Your Partner."

Practice 2 を参考にして、質問に答えましょう。"You" の下には自分の答えを書き、そのあとパートナーに質問して、答えを "Your Partner" の下に書きましょう。

Question	You	Your Partner
1. What kind of music do you like?		
2. Who's your favorite singer or group?		
3. What kind of music do you dislike?		
4. What kind of TV programs do you like?		
5. What's your favorite TV program?		
6. What kind of TV programs do you dislike?		
7. What kind of movies do you like?		
8. What's your favorite movie?		
9. What kind of movies do you dislike?		
10. What's your favorite sport?		
11. Who's your favorite athlete?*		
12. What sports do you dislike?		

* entertainment 娯楽　　athlete スポーツマン、運動選手

Grammar 1

39

Gerunds and Infinitives

動名詞と不定詞

When talking about activities we like or dislike, we use either gerunds (～ ing) or infinitives (to do) after like / love.

行動や活動についての好き嫌いを説明するときは、like / love のあとに動名詞（～ ing）か不定詞（to do）を使います。

Let's talk about likes and dislikes for different kinds of actions.

ここでは、さまざまな行動や活動（動詞）の好き嫌いを表してみましょう。

Gerunds

動名詞　～ ing

I love ***playing*** tennis.
I like ***eating*** at restaurants.
I don't like ***reading*** comic books.
I dislike ***driving***.

I hate ***doing*** homework.

Infinitives

不定詞　to + 動詞の原形

I love ***to play*** tennis.
I like ***to eat*** at restaurants.
I don't like ***to read*** comic books.
~~I dislike to drive.~~
(“dislike” は to 不定詞とは使えません)
I hate ***to do*** homework.

▶Practice 4 Writing: Questions and Answers ライティング：自分について答えよう

Write short answers that are true for you.

自分のことについて答えてみましょう

Example: A: Do you like cooking?
B: Yes, I do. I love it.

1. A: Do you like to play online games?
   B: ______________________
2. A: Do you like to do homework?
   B: ______________________
3. A: Do you like cooking?
   B: ______________________
4. A: Do you like taking tests?
   B: ______________________

▶Practice 5 Writing ライティング

Complete the sentences to make true statements about what you like and do not like to do. Use the gerund form when there is no "to."

自分の好き嫌いについて、以下の５つの文を完成させてください。"to" がないときは、" ～ ing" 形を使いましょう。

1. I love ______________________________
2. I like to ______________________________
3. I don't like to ______________________________
4. I dislike ______________________________
5. I hate to ______________________________

Grammar 2

40

Agreeing and Disagreeing

同意する、しない

Agreeing 同意する

A: I love ice cream.
B: So do I*.

A: I like to watch TV.
B: So do I.

A: I don't like blue cheese.
B: Neither do I*.

A: I hate horror movies.
B: So do I.

Disagreeing 同意しない

A: I love Korean pop music.
B: Oh, I don't.

A: I like pancakes.
B: I don't.

A: I don't like *sushi.*
B: Oh, I do. I love it.

A: I hate romance movies.
B: Oh really? I love them.

*so do I 私も～です　　neither do I 私も～ない

▶Practice 6 Matching 質問に合った答えをさがそう

Put the correct letters for the answers in the space.

1～8までの質問に対する最も適切な答えをA～Hの中から選びましょう。

______ 1. I like ice cream.	A. Apples.
______ 2. I hate horror movies.	B. So do I. Chocolate is my favorite flavor.
______ 3. I'm crazy about cats.	C. Really? I love them, especially* cookies.
______ 4. I don't like sweets.	D. I don't. I don't like snow.
______ 5. What's your favorite fruit?	E. I like rock music.
______ 6. I love skiing.	F. I don't. I can't eat raw fish*.
______ 7. I like *sushi.*	G. So do I. They scare* me.
______ 8. What kind of music do you like?	H. I'm not. I like dogs more*.

* especially 特に　raw fish 生魚、刺身　scare 怖がらせる　more ～より～

▶Practice 7 Listening リスニング 41

Listen to the following conversation and write in the missing words.

会話文を聞いて空欄を埋めましょう。

Matt: What kind of things do you ____________________ on weekends?

Mari: I ____________________. I really ____________________ volleyball.

Matt: ____________________, but I ____________________ basketball.

Mari: That's great! Do you ____________________ TV?

Matt: Yes, I ____________________ sports on TV.

Mari: I don't. I like ____________________, though*.

Matt: What's ____________________ drama?

Mari: *Attack of the Zombies.*

Matt: Really? I ____________ horror movies.

* though（文末に使われた場合）～だけどね

▶Practice 8 Writing ライティング

First, write down your feelings about the things or activities below. Use as many different phrases as you can (I like, I really like, I don't like, I hate, etc.). Also, use the verbs in some sentences to make gerunds or infinitives.

次の活動についての自分の気持ちを話してみましょう。できるだけ多く異なるフレーズ (I like, I really like, I don't like, I hate, etc.) を使ってください。また、動名詞や不定詞も使ってみてください。

Example: I like playing the piano. (play the piano)

1. ______________________________ (take tests)

2. ______________________________ (cats)

3. ______________________________ (study)

4. ______________________________ (run)

5. ______________________________ (travel)

6. ______________________________ (fly)

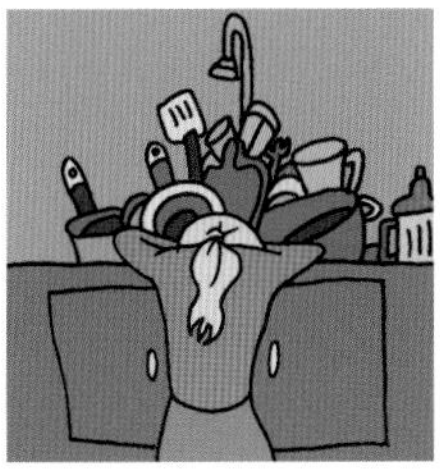

7. ______________________________ (wash dishes)

8. ______________________________ (broccoli)

Now talk to your partner and see if she / he agrees or disagrees with you.
相手が自分と同意見かどうかを聞いてみましょう。例を参考にしてください。

Example: Student A: I don't like rock music.
Student B: Really? I do.

▶Practice 9 Entertainment Survey (2) 娯楽についてのインタビュー (2) 42

Choose one type of entertainment to write your survey about (sports, music, TV, video games, etc.). Write five questions. Then ask your questions to five students in the class. Finally, prepare to share what you learned in your survey.
娯楽（スポーツ、音楽、テレビ、ビデオゲームなど）の中からひとつ選びそれに関する質問を作ってみましょう。例を参考にして質問を５問作り､５人のクラスメイトに聞いてみましょう。最後にそのインタビューでわかったことをシェアしてください。

Examples: About TV

Questions	Answers
1. What kind of TV programs do you like?	I like music shows.
2. Who's your favorite actor?	I love ...
3. What's your favorite program?	I like ...
4. Why do you like it?	I like it because it's ...
5. When do you watch TV?	I usually watch in the evenings.

＊ often 頻繁に

Type of Entertainment: ____________________

Questions

1. ____________________?
2. ____________________?
3. ____________________?
4. ____________________?
5. ____________________?

Answers

Name	Notes
1.	
2.	
3.	
4.	
5.	

Review Units 4 - 6

Unit 4 から Unit 6 までの復習

▶Practice 1 Crossword クロスワード

Work in pairs. **Student A:** Look at this page. **Student B:** Turn to **Appendix 5**. Give hints to help your partner guess the words that you can see in your half of the crossword. But do not say the actual words in your hints. Then listen to your partner and write in the words that he / she is describing.

Student A はこのページを，Student B は Appendix 5 を見てください。それぞれのクロスワードですでに 埋まっている単語をパートナーにあててもらいます。ヒントを出し合い，お互いのクロスワードの空欄を埋めましょう。 答 えを言ってしまわないように気を付けて。

Example: A: What's 2 down?
B: It's a word for a family member. Your mother's daughter is your ...?
A: "Sister"?
A: That's right! Now, what's 1 across?
B: It's the part of your body you use to see.
A: Is it "eyes"?
B: Yes. Well done!

Student A

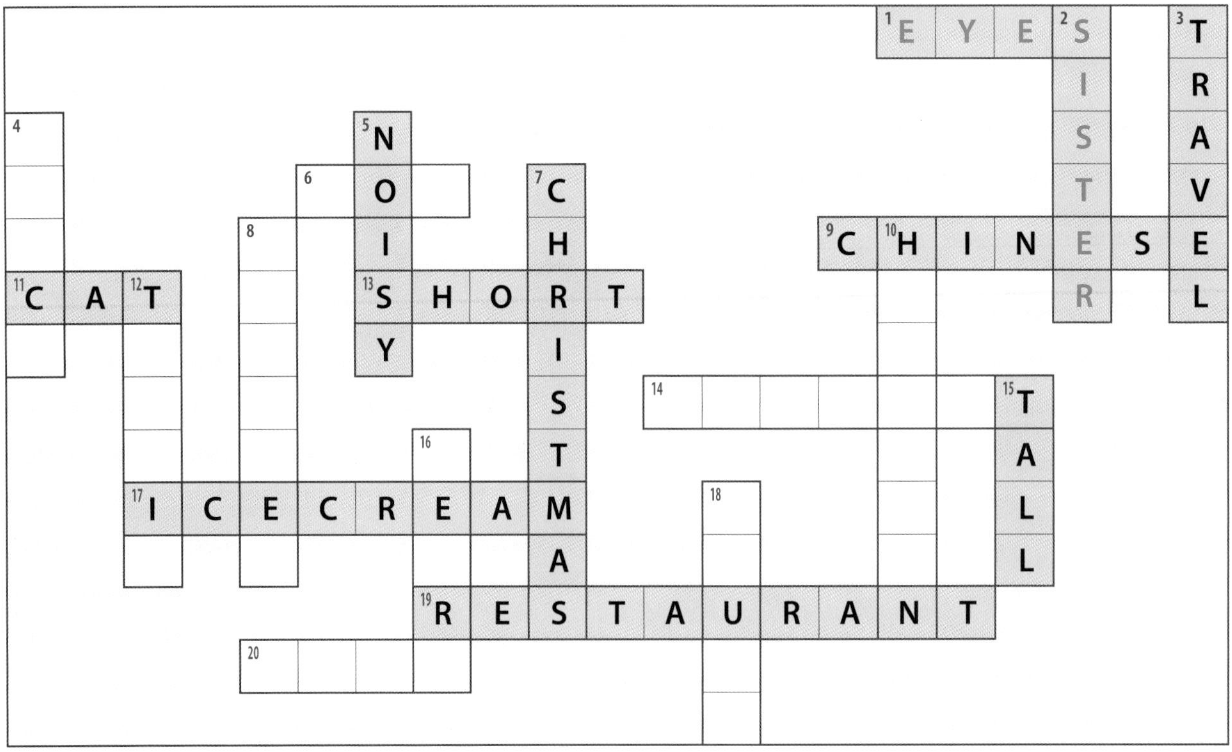

▶Practice 2 Pair Work: Likes and Dislikes Game ペアワーク：好き嫌いゲーム

In pairs try to find as many similarities in your likes and dislikes as possible. Use as many different phrases as you can (I like, I really like, I don't like, I hate, etc.). Each time you find a match, you get one point. You have 5 minutes!

自分とパートナーの好き嫌いについて、共通点をたくさん探してみましょう。I like, I really like, I don't like, I hate などの表現を使ってみましょう。共通点をひとつ見つけたら１ポイントになります。制限時間は５分です！

Example: Student A: "I like ice cream. And you?"
Student B: "So do I. / I like ice cream, too." (One point)

Now play the same game again with a different partner. But this time try to find differences in likes and dislikes. Each time you find a difference, you get one point.

次は、別のパートナーと同じゲームをしてみましょう。でも今度はパートナーとの好き嫌いの相違点を探します。相違点をひとつ見つけたら１ポイントです。

Example: Student A: "I like baseball. And you?"
Student B: "Oh, I don't." (One point)

Unit 7

Personality

性格

Speaking スピーキング

Practice the following dialogues with a partner. After you have practiced the model conversation a few times, substitute the underlined information with the words in the boxes.

以下の会話をパートナーと練習してください。数回練習したら、下線の部分を枠内の表現に言いかえて再度練習しください。

Dialogue 1 43

Chen: What's your father like, Reina?

Reina: He's very kind.(1) But he's shy. He doesn't talk much.

Chen: And your mother?

Reina: Oh, she's strict*. How about your parents, Chen?

Chen: Well, I'm sometimes stubborn,* (2) but my parents are patient* with me. I respect* them.

1. intelligent*	2. selfish*

Dialogue 2 44

Mark: What's your dog like. Yumi?

Yumi: He's friendly.(1) He likes everybody. Do you have a pet?

Mark: Our family has a cat. She's unfriendly.* (2) She often fights with other cats and dogs.

Yumi: That's too bad.

1. sweet*	2. mean*

*strict 厳しい　stubborn 頑固な　patient 我慢強い　respect 尊敬する　intelligent 知的な
selfish 自分勝手な　unfriendly よそよそしい　sweet 優しい　mean いじわるな

▶Practice 1 Personality Words 性格を表す表現

Put the words in the box that describe personality under the correct picture.

次の絵を最もよく表す表現を枠内から選びましょう。

selfish	friendly	stubborn	intelligent	positive	
strict	negative	emotional	helpful	silly	honest

1. ____________________

2. ____________________

3. ____________________

4. ____________________

5. ____________________

6. ____________________

7. ____________________

8. ____________________

9. ____________________

10. ____________________

11. ____________________

▶Practice 2 Positive and Negative Characteristics (1) ポジティブな特徴とネガティブな特徴 (1)

Look at the words below. Put the opposite meanings in the chart.

表に書き込まれた単語と反対の意味を表す単語を、枠内から選んで書き入れましょう。

boring kind careful dishonest stubborn
unintelligent helpful positive friendly

	Positive Meaning	Negative Meaning
1.	honest	
2.		careless
3.	exciting	
4.		unkind
5.	intelligent	
6.		unfriendly
7.		unhelpful
8.	flexible	
9.		negative

▶Practice 3 Positive and Negative Characteristics (2) ポジティブな特徴とネガティブな特徴 (2)

Look at the words from Practice 2 and write them in the correct spaces below.

空欄に合う形容詞を、Practice 2 の表から選んで入れましょう。

1. Thank you so much for giving me such a nice birthday present. That was so _______________ of you.
2. **Tina:** May I copy your homework?
   Misaki: No, that's _______________. Please do your homework by yourself*.
3. Many students at this university smile and say "hello" to me. They are so _______________ (not "kind").
4. This class is too easy for me, so it's _______________.
5. Erica made many mistakes on her report. I think she's a little _______________.
6. Wow, you got the highest score in our class. You're so _______________.
7. **Jun:** I don't like to study. I never do well, anyway.
   Jon: Don't be so _______________. You'll do better if you study.

*by yourself ひとりで

8. Kevin never listens to me, even though I try to help him. He's so ______________.
9. GPS is very ______________ when you go to a new place. It makes finding places very easy.

Grammar 1

Comparative and Superlative Adjectives

比較級 (Comparative) と最上級 (Superlative)

Usually, comparative adjectives end in "...er" and superlative adjectives end in "...est". Also, "than" is added after comparative adjectives and "the" is added before superlative adjectives.
通常、比較級は原級の形容詞に "er" を付け、そのあとに "than" を入れます。最上級は形容詞に "est" を付け、その前に "the" を入れます。

Adjective 形容詞	Comparative 比較級	Superlative 最上級
Beth is ***smart***.*	She's ***smarter than*** me.	She's ***the smartest*** in her family.
Ivan is ***tall***.	He's ***taller than*** me.	He's ***the tallest*** student in my class.

Adjectives ending with "y" end with "-ier" to make the comparative and "-iest" to make the superlative.
"y" で終わっている形容詞で "y" の前が子音の場合は、"y" を "i" に変えて、"er" を付けて比較級を作り、最上級を作るときは、"est" を付けます。

Easy ⇨	English is ***easier than*** French.	Is English ***the easiest*** language in the world?
Friendly ⇨	Karla is ***friendlier than*** her sister.	She's ***the friendliest*** person I know.

Most longer adjectives don't change in the comparative and superlative forms, but "more" is added before comparative adjectives and "the most" is added before superlative adjectives.
２音節の形容詞（例外もある）や、３音節以上の形容詞を比較級にするには "more"、最上級には "the most" を付けます。

She's ***more intelligent**** than me.
Math is ***the most difficult*** class.
Ms. Evans is ***the most patient*** teacher at our school.

Some adjectives are irregular in their comparative and superlative forms.
比較級、最上級が不規則に変化する形容詞もあります。

good	**better**	**best**
bad	**worse**	**worst**
many	**more**	**most**

*smart 頭のよい　intelligent 知的な

▶Practice 4 Comparatives and Superlatives 比較級と最上級

Write three sentences, the first sentence with the given adjective, then the second with the comparative, and the third with the superlative forms of the adjective.

以下の絵を表わす形容詞を使って文をつくり、その形容詞を比較級と最上級にした文をひとつずつ作りましょう。例を参考にひとつの形容詞につき３文作ってください。

Example: kind

Yohei

Yohei is kind.

Shannon

Shannon is kinder than Yohei.

Abdullah

Abdullah is the kindest.

1. shy*

Bart

Kim

Erin

2. strict*

My mother

My brother

My father

*shy 恥ずかしがり屋の　strict 厳しい

3. intelligent*

Vance

Lina

James

4. scary*

Godzilla

Frankenstein

Dracula

5. stubborn*

My younger brother

My younger sister

My father

*intelligent 知的な　scary 怖い　stubborn 頑固な

▶Practice 5 Listening リスニング 45

Listen to a person talk about his sister. Write in the missing words.

旅行ライターになりたいと思っている人の話を聞いて、空欄を埋めましょう。

My sister, Barbara, is ______________________________ in my family. She's helpful and often does volunteer work* at a school ______________________________. She tutors* ________ ________________ who need help. She knows how to help them _________________________. She's ______________________________ am. She ______________________________ and she understands her students' feelings*.

Sometimes her ______________________ and they do ________________ study. But ________ ________________ and patient* with them. She's ____________________________ person I know. She listens to her students and supports them. That's why* ______________________________ the school.

* volunteer work ボランティアの仕事　tutor 個人指導する　feelings 気持ち
patient 我慢強い　that's why だから、そういう理由で

▶Practice 6 World Quiz ワールドクイズ 46

Read the questions and circle the correct answer, as in the example.

質問を読んで正しい答えを丸で囲みましょう。(check)

Example: What's the longest river?

A. The Mekong

B. The Nile

C. The Mississippi

1. Which people live the longest?

A. Americans

B. Japanese

C. Germans

2. Which country is the biggest (in size)?

A. China

B. Canada

C. Russia

3. Which country has the most people?

A. Russia

B. America

C. India

4. What's the highest mountain in the world?

A. Mount Everest

B. Mount Kilimanjaro

C. The Matterhorn

5. Which country had the first Olympics?

A. Italy

B. Greece

C. Egypt

6. Which animals are the fastest?

A. Cheetahs

B. Elephants

C. Horses

▶Practice 7 Kenta and His Robots Kentaとロボット

First, look at the pictures below that describe the story. Choose the sentence that best describes the picture and write letters (A, B, C ...) in the boxes above the pictures so that the sentences are in the correct order.

以下の絵を表す内容をA～Kの中から選び、四角の中に入れましょう。

A. Kenta is 24 years old and is a businessman. He makes a robot called Rob that he can be friends with. Rob welcomes Kenta home from work every day.

B. Kenta is 14 years old. He makes four more robots in different shapes and colors.

C. His second robot can do many more things. The robot wins a contest, so Kenta is very happy.

D. Kenta makes one very big robot. He doesn't like this robot, because it looks scary* and is dangerous*.

E. Kenta and Rob talk about many things together. Kenta is never lonely* when he comes home from work.

F. Kenta becomes very old. His legs are weak* and he cannot walk. Rob helps him. Kenta is very happy to have such a good friend.

G. Kenta makes a robot with four arms. The robot is very helpful.

H. Kenta is very intelligent. He likes to make things. He is just eight years old. He made his first robot. It is simple. It has no legs, but it can move.

I. He makes many more robots. Some of them look like people, but some look like animals. Some can even fly.

J. Kenta is 12 years old. He makes a very intelligent robot. The robot talks with him.

K. Kenta makes a robot that is silly and funny. He sometimes takes this robot to parties to make people laugh.

*scary 怖い　dangerous 危ない　lonely 寂しい　weak 弱い

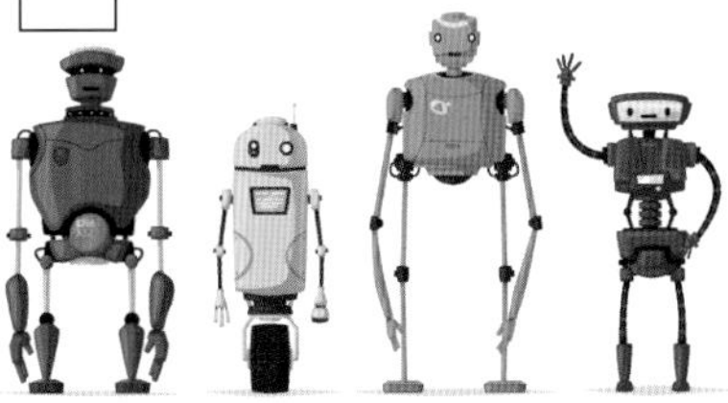

*smart 賢い　boring つまらない

▶Practice 8 Writing ライティング

Write about the personality of someone you know, such as a friend, a family member, or even yourself. You can look at Practice 1, 2, and 5 for ideas. When you are finished, be ready to share your description with a group or the whole class.

練習 1, 2, 5 を参考にして、友人や家族、あるいは自分の性格について書いてみましょう。書き終わったら、それをクラスメイトやグループでシェアする準備をしましょう。

Unit 8

Tell Me About Your Family

家族について教えて

Speaking スピーキング

Practice the following dialogues with a partner. After you have practiced the model conversation a few times, substitute the underlined information with the words in the boxes.

以下の会話をパートナーと練習してください。数回練習したら、下線の部分を枠内の表現に言いかえて再度練習しください。

Dialogue 1 47

Steve: How many people are there in your family, Mayu?

Mayu: There are four, my father, my mother, my sister,(1) and me.

Steve: Is your sister(1) older or younger than you?

Mayu: She's(2) three years younger(3) than me.

1. brother	2. He's	3. older

Dialogue 2 48

Steve: What does your father do?

Mayu: He's an engineer.*(1) He works for a large company in Osaka.

Steve: And your mother?

Mayu: She's a writer.(2) What about your family, Steve?

Steve: There are only three of us. I'm an only child.* Both my parents are teachers.(3)

1. a salesman*	2. nurse	3. lawyers*

*engineer エンジニア　only child 一人っ子　salesman セールスマン　lawyer 弁護士

Grammar 1

There is + singular / There are + plural

～がある（モノ）、～がいる（人、動物）

There is ＋ 単数／There are ＋ 複数

How much milk ***is there***?	***There's*** a lot of milk in the refrigerator*.
How many people ***are there*** in your family?	(***They're***) Five.
How many students ***are there*** in your class?	(***They're***) 28.
Is there any homework?	Yes, ***there is***.
Are there any pencils?	Yes, ***there are some*** on the desk.
Is there any milk?	No, ***there isn't***.
Are there any bananas?	No, ***there aren't***.

*refrigerator 冷蔵庫

▶Practice 1 Matching 質問に合った答えをさがそう

Put the letter for the correct answer next to each question.

1～6までの質問の答えとして、最も適切なものをA～Fから選びましょう。

_____	1. How many people are there in your family?	A. Yes, I do. I have one brother and two sisters.
_____	2. How old is your brother?	B. He's 20. He's in college.
_____	3. Do you have any brothers or sisters?	C. There are three. I'm an only child.
_____	4. What does your father do?	D. He's very serious*. He studies a lot.
_____	5. What's your mother like?	E. She's very funny. She likes to tell jokes*.
_____	6. What's your brother like?	F. He's a doctor.

*serious まじめな　　tell jokes 冗談を言う

Grammar 2

50

Count / Noncount Nouns

数えられる名詞 / 数えられない名詞

In English, some nouns can be counted (count nouns), while other nouns cannot be counted (noncount nouns). Plural count nouns usually have an "s" at the end.

数えられない名詞は、複数でも単数として扱い、数えられる名詞の複数形には "s" を付けますが、数えられない名詞の複数形には "s" を付けません。(例：people)

Count nouns 数えられる名詞：

There ***is one student*** in the classroom.
There ***are ten books*** on my desk.
There ***are five people*** in my family.
There ***are*** no good ***movies*** on TV tonight.
There ***are a few apples***.
There ***are a lot of / many people*** in the station.

Noncount nouns 数えられない名詞：形が決まっていないもの（入れ物や切り方などによって 形が変わる）や 抽象的な概念など

This ***is some milk***.
There ***is no homework*** today.
There ***is a little milk***.
This ***is a lot of / much tea***.

▶Practice 2 Grammar: Find the Mistakes 文法：間違いをさがそう

Find the mistakes in the following sentences and correct them. The first one is done for you.

1～6までの文を正しい文に書き換えましょう。1は例です。

1. There is five people in my family. *There are five people in my family.*
2. I have four families, my parents, my brother, and me. ____________________
   ____
3. How many milks do we have? ____________________
4. I like to watch movie in my free time. ____________________
5. There have many student in my class. ____________________
6. There is much apples. ____________________

▶Practice 3 Grammar 文法

Answer the following questions using "There is...." And "There are...".

以下の質問に、There is/There are で答えましょう。

1. Are there any books?

   Answer: ____

2. How many books are there?

   Answer: ____

3. How many people are there in the family?

   Answer: ____

4. Are there any dishes on the table?

   Answer: ____

5. Is there any tea in the teapot?

   Answer: ____

6. How many students are there in the classroom?

   Answer: ____

Key Words 51

Family Members 家族、親戚

mother　father　aunt 叔母　uncle 伯父　grandfather 祖父　grandmother 祖母
grandparents 祖父母　grandson 孫息子　granddaughter 孫娘　grandchildren 孫
son 息子　daughter 娘　brother 兄 / 弟　sister 姉 / 妹　cousin いとこ　niece 姪
nephew 甥　husband 夫　wife 妻　parents 親　children 子供たち

▶Practice 4　Family Tree (1)　家系図 (1)

Look at Lisa's family tree. Write in the missing words from the Key Words to complete the tree.

空欄を埋めて、Lisa の家系図を完成させましょう。

▶Practice 5 Matching: Relatives 空欄を埋めよう：家族、親戚

Put the correct letters A-H in the spaces to complete the sentences.

1～8までの空欄に入る最も適切なものをA～Hから選びましょう。

1. My son's son is my _______.
2. My mother's sister is my _______.
3. My uncle's son is my _______.
4. My mother's mother is my _______.
5. The man I married is my _______.
6. My mother's husband is my _______.
7. The brother of my father is my _______.
8. My sister's daughter is my _______.

A. aunt
B. grandmother
C. husband
D. niece
E. grandson
F. father
G. cousin
H. uncle

▶Practice 6 Family Words Bingo ファミリーメンバー・ビンゴ 52

Select 16 words from the Key Words (Family Members) box on page 87 and write them in the bingo card below.

87ページのKey Words家族/親戚を表す単語から16個を選び、ビンゴカードに記入しましょう。

Now listen to your teacher describe different family members. You must listen carefully because you won't hear the actual words, but hints that help you guess the words. Cross off the words corresponding to the hints. When you have crossed off four words in a row on your card, shout "Bingo!"

先生が家族/親戚について説明します。ヒントをよく聞いて，当てはまる単語があれば消していきます。4つ消すことができたら、大きな声で"Bingo!"と言いましょう。

▶Practice 7 Family Tree (2) 家系図 (2)

Student A: Stay on this page. **Student B**: Turn to **Appendix 6**. There are 11 differences in Trevor's family tree. Ask questions to each other to find the differences.

Student A はこのページを見てください。Student B は Appendix 6 を見てください。2 人の見ている Trevor の家系図には 11 か所異なる点があります。お互いに質問しながら違いを見つけましょう。

Examples: Who is Janice married to? What does Trevor do?
How old is Richard's wife? What's Richard's wife's name?

*retired 退職者

▶Practice 8 Listening リスニング 53

Listen to someone talk about their family. Fill in the missing words.

家族について話している人の話を聞いて、空欄を埋めましょう。

There ________________ in my family, my mother, my father, my brother, my __________ ________________. My father is retired, ____________________ still works. She's a caretaker* at a retirement home*. She's ____________________ helps people. My brother is __________________. He's __________________ and works in a bank. He's very serious and he always ________________. We __________________. My sister is __________________. She's 17 and is a senior __________________. She's smart and she ____________________. She loves computers and _______________ a software engineer* in the future. Our family ___ ______________. _____________ Brutus. He's ______________ noisy*.

* caretaker 介護士　retirement home 老人ホーム　software engineer ソフトウェア エンジニア　noisy（音などが）うるさい

▶Practice 9 Family Tree (3) 家系図 (3)

Draw your own family tree (like the one in Practice 4 and 7) on a piece of paper. Then write some sentences about your family below.

Practice 4 と 7 の家系図を参考に、自分の家系図を書き、そのあと家族のメンバーについて以下に説明文を書いてみましょう。

▶Practice 10 Find Someone Who ... こんな人を探そう

First, complete the questions on the left of the chart below. Then find someone who answers "yes" to the questions and write their names on the right. Try to talk to as many people as you can.

表の左側の質問を完成させ、それに Yes（否定の質問で聞かれたら答えは No）と答えられる人を見つけ右側の空欄に記入してください。できるだけたくさんの人に聞いてみましょう。

Example: Find someone who has a strict mother or father.
Question: Is your mother or father strict?
Answer: Yes, my father is strict. (Write down the person's name)

Find Someone ...	Name
1. ... who has a younger sister. Question: ____________________?	
2. ... who has an older brother. Question: ____________________?	
3. ... who is an only child. Question: ____________________?	
4. ... who has a strict mother or father. Question: ____________________?	
5. ... who wants to have a child in the future. Question: ____________________?	
6. ... who has a family pet. Question: ____________________?	

Grammar 2

54

Modal Verbs: Should and Must

助動詞：“should” と ”must”

“Should” and “must” are followed by the main verbs of sentences. “Should” is used for advice while “must” is used for necessity. Therefore, “must” is stronger.

“should” と “must” は、そのあとに動詞の原形が必要です。“should” はアドバイスをするときのように、〜したほうが良い、という意味合いで、“must” は〜しなければならないという意味で使われるため、“must” のほうが強い印象を与えます。

Children ***should*** help their parents with housework.*
Students ***shouldn't*** sleep in class.
I ***must*** study this weekend.
Small children ***mustn't*** run into the street.

*housework 家事

▶Practice 11 Group Work グループワーク

In groups, write down some things that make a good parent (mother and/or father). Use the modals *should*, *shouldn't*, *must*, and *mustn't* as shown in the grammar examples above.

グループで「良い親（父親や母親）」の条件とは何か考え、上記の例文を参考に、should/shouldn't, must/mustn't, を使って文章を書いてみましょう。

Example: Parents should give their children healthy food.
Parents mustn't give their children too much junk food.

1.
2.
3.
4.
5.
6.
7.
8.

▶Practice 12 Missing Words 穴埋め練習

Look at the presentation below. Choose the correct words from the box and write them in the spaces below.

次のプレゼンテーションの空欄に入る最も適切な単語を、枠内から選びましょう。

like	loves	listening	draws	senior	older
animation	much	brown	everybody		

Hello, ____________. Today, I'd like to talk about my ____________ brother. He's 21 years old and is a ____________ in university. He's tall and has short ____________ hair. He's interesting and funny. He doesn't ____________ to study but I think he's intelligent. He's crazy about* comics and ________________. He sometimes writes and ____________ his own comics. His favorite movie is Totoro. He also ____________ Korean pop music. I like my brother very ____________. Thank you for ____________.

* crazy about～ ～に夢中

▶Practice 13 Presentation プレゼンテーション

You will give a presentation about someone you know—a friend, a family member, or another person. Write sentences about their appearance, personality, and any other information you think is important to understand them. After writing your description, practice it so that you can look at your audience when speaking.

さあ、今度はみなさんが友達や家族の誰かを紹介する番です。見た目や性格、その他の情報について文を書いてください。書き終わったら、実際にプレゼンテーションをする前に、クラスメイトたちとアイコンタクトをとりながら話せるように練習しましょう。

Unit 9

Feelings

気持ちを表す

Speaking スピーキング

Practice the following dialogues with a partner. After you have practiced the model conversation a few times, substitute the underlined information with the words in the boxes.

以下の会話をパートナーと練習してください。数回練習したら、下線の部分を枠内の表現に言いかえて再度練習しください。

Dialogue 1 55

Emi: How are you, Carlos? You look tired.[1]

Carlos: Yeah, I am. I studied until 2 a.m. this morning. I have a big test this afternoon.

Emi: Are you worried about* it?

Carlos: Yes, I am. The class isn't easy for me and I often get confused.*[2]

Emi: Well, good luck.

Carlos: Thanks.

1. sleepy	2. stressed

* worry about ~ ~について心配する、悩む　confused 混乱する

Dialogue 2 (The Next Day) 56

Emi: What's up*, Carlos? You look unhappy[1]!

Carlos: The test was so difficult. I was really surprised.[2]

Emi: Did you get a bad score?

Carlos: Yes. I only got 38 points, so I didn't pass.*

Emi: That's too bad.

1. down*	2. shocked

* What's up? どうしたの？　pass 合格する　down 落ち込んでいる

▶Practice 1 Matching どんな気持ち？ 57

Put the words in the box that best describe how the characters are feeling.

それぞれの絵がどんな感情を表しているかを枠内から選びましょう。

angry 怒って surprised 驚く bored 退屈する sad 悲しい sleepy
jealous うらやましい disappointed がっかりする proud 誇りに思う
shy 恥ずかしがりやの scared 怖い excited わくわくする confused 混乱した

1. ______________________

2. ______________________

3. ______________________

4. ______________________

5. ______________________

6. ______________________

7. ______________________

8. ______________________

9. ______________________

10. ______________________

11. ______________________

12. ______________________

Grammar 1

58

Asking about and Expressing Feelings

相手の気持ちを聞く、自分の感情を表す

Questions:	**Answers:**
How are you (feeling)?	I'm alright.
Is everything OK / alright?	Yeah, fine.
Are you OK?	Yes, but I'm tired.
You look happy. What's up?	I just got an "A" on my test.
What's wrong?	I'm angry at my sister.
What's the matter?	I'm worried about today's test.

▶Practice 2 How Are You Feeling? 気分はどう？

Choose the correct words from the box below to complete the sentence. More than one answer may be possible.

感情を表す最も適切な表現を枠内から選んで文章を完成させましょう。答えは必ずしもひとつとは限りません。

scared excited worried confused interested 興味がある
bored disappointed surprised

1. **Mother:** How's your math* class?
   Tim: It's not interesting, so I often get ________________.
2. **Sarah:** Why do you want to join the English club?
   Ai: Because I'm really ________________ in English.
3. **Marina:** How was the baseball game?
   Doug: My team lost. I'm so ________________.
4. **Penny:** Why do you look so happy, Adam?
   Adam: I'm really ________________ because I'm going to a concert this afternoon.
5. **Kay:** I don't understand this math problem. I'm ________________.
   Jun: I see. I'll help you, then.
6. **Shoko:** Did you enjoy your birthday party?
   Hana: Yes, I did. Nobody told me about it, so I was really ________________.
7. **Shun:** How was the movie?
   Lisa: It was a horror movie. I was so ________________.
8. **Steve:** What's wrong*, Cathy?
   Cathy: My grandmother is in the hospital. I'm so ________________.

*math (mathematics) 数学　What's wrong? どうしたの？

Grammar 2

Adjectives with "-ed" and "-ing"

現在分詞（動詞の ~ing 形）や動詞の過去分詞（～ ed 形など）を形容詞として使う

When we talk about feelings, we often use adjectives that end in "ed", such as "I'm surpris**ed**." We use the "ed" ending when the feeling is inside us. When we talk about an outside event that gives us a feeling, we often use an "ing" ending, such as "The news is surpris**ing**."

人の感情を表すときに、現在分詞（動詞の～ ing 形）や過去分詞（動詞の過去分詞形～ ed など）を形容詞として使うことがあります。自分の感情を表すときは、過去分詞（I'm surpris**ed**. など）を使い、「何かが、自分にある感情を起こさせる」場合や、ある事象の説明をするときは、現在分詞（The news is surpris**ing** など）を使います。

I am ～ ed. He / She is ～ ed. We / They are ～ ed.（過去分詞を形容詞のように使う）

interested, surprised, excited, bored*, disappointed, confused, relaxed

It is ～ ing. （現在分詞を形容詞のように使う）

interesting, surprising, exciting, boring*, disappointing, surprising, confusing, relaxing

*bored / boring つまらない

►Practice 3 How Does It Make You Feel? どんな気持ちになる？

Look back at your answers to questions 1-5 in Practice 2. They all used the '~ed' pattern to explain each person's feelings. Now use the '~ing' pattern to explain how the outside event made each person feel.

Practice 2の１から５までの答えを見てください。すべて過去分詞（～ed）を使って感情を表しています。今度は、現在分詞（～ing）を使って気持ちを表してみましょう。

1. Tim isn't interested in his math class because it's ______________________________.
2. Ai wants to join the English club because she thinks English is ________________________.
3. Doug's baseball team lost and he said it's ______________________________.
4. Adam thinks the concert will be ______________________________.
5. Kay says the math problem is ______________________________.

►Practice 4 Feeling Words 感情を表す表現

Complete the following sentences with the correct words describing feelings. Use the correct form of the "be" verb in the present tense.

それぞれの絵を表す感情表現を枠内から選んで、空欄に入れましょう。正しい be 動詞を入れるのを忘れずに。

disappointed confusing surprising
scared bored disappointing surprised
boring scary confused

Example:
He ***is excited*** because the concert ***is exciting***.

1. She ________________________ because the movie ________________________.

2. I ________________________ because the software program ________________________.

3. He ______________________ because the news ______________________.

4. They ______________________ because the class ______________________.

5. She ______________________ because her grade* ______________________.

* grade 成績

▶Practice 5 Your Feelings 自分の気持ち

Write answers to the following questions about your feelings.

質問に対するあなたの気持ちを書きましょう。

Example: How do you feel when you have a difficult test?
I feel stressed.

1. How do you feel when you get a bad score on a test?

____

2. How do you feel when you get a present?

____

3. How do you feel when you study until late at night?

____

4. How do you feel when someone is mean* to you?

____

5. How do you feel when you watch a horror movie?

____

＊mean 意地悪な

▶Practice 6 Gesture Game ジェスチャーゲーム

Your teacher will give you feeling words to act out in groups. Try to get other students to guess the word. Use gestures and facial expressions only.

グループを作り、一人がジェスチャーで気持ちを表します。ほかのメンバーはクラスメイトの気持ちを英語であてます。表情とジェスチャーのみで気持ちを表してください。

Example: A: (Uses gestures or expressions on his/her face to describe a feeling.)
ジェスチャーや顔の表情であなたの気持ちを表しましょう。
B: Are you sad?
A: No, I'm not sad.
C: Are you angry?
A: Yes, I'm angry!

▶Practice 7 My Feelings 私の気持ち

Part A

Complete the sentences below, describing when you feel the emotions. Number 1 has been done for you.

次の感情を感じるときはどんなときですか？文章を完成させましょう。

1. I feel sad when I *get a bad grade.*
2. I feel happy when I ______________________________
3. I get excited when I ______________________________
4. I feel nervous when I ______________________________
5. I feel scared when I ______________________________

Part B

Now, work in pairs. Take turns asking questions about the emotions in Part A. Use the expression "When do you feel ...?"

Part A の感情について、パートナーと順番に質問しあいましょう。"When do you feel ...?" という表現を使って質問文をつくりましょう。

> **Example:** A: When do you feel excited?
> B: I feel excited when I go to a concert.

▶Practice 8 Find Someone Who ... こんな人を探そう

First, complete the questions on the left of the chart below. Then find someone who answers "yes" to the questions and write their names on the right. Try to talk to as many people as you can.

表の左側の質問を完成させ、それに Yes（否定の質問で聞かれたら答えは No）と答えられる人を見つけ右側の空欄に記入してください。できるだけたくさんの人に聞いてみましょう。

> **Example:** Find someone who gets excited watching sports.
> Question: Do you get excited watching sports?
> Answer: Yes, I do. (Write down the person's name)

Find someone who ...	**Name**
1. ... feels sleepy now. Question: ________________________?	
2. ... sometimes gets angry. Question: ________________________?	
3. ... is nervous before a test. Question: ________________________?	
4. ... gets excited watching sports. Question: ________________________?	
5. ... is sometimes bored in class. Question: ________________________?	
6. ... cries during a sad movie. Question: ________________________?	

▶Practice 9 Drawing 表情を描いてみよう 59

Choose five emotions. Draw faces with these emotions in the circles. Show them to your partner. Ask them to guess what the emotions are.

5つの感情を選んで、丸枠の中にそれを表わす表情を描きましょう。例を参考にパートナーにそれらがどんな感情かを聞いて下さい。

Example: Student A: What emotion is this?
Student B: Is it "angry"?
Student A: No, it isn't "angry." Guess again!
Student B: Is it "nervous*"?
Student A: Yes, that's right! It's nervous.

1

2

3

4

5

* nervous 緊張している

Review Units 7 - 9

Unit 7 から Unit 9 までの復習

▶Practice 1 Listening: Date Your Dream リスニング：理想のデートの相手 60 61

Jessie is on a show called "Date Your Dream." Listen to three men and Jessie talk about themselves. Takes notes in the chart below. Which man is the best date for Jessie?

Jessie は "Date Your Dream" というテレビ番組に出演しています。3 人の男性と Jessie との会話を聞いて下の表にメモを取りましょう。Jessie に一番合う相手は誰でしょう？

Jessie

Key Words

professor 教授　**book-loving** 読書が好きな　**social media** SNS
nervous 緊張する、神経質な

	Tim	Bart	Craig	Jessie
Job				
Age				
Personality				
Likes				
Dislikes				

Best Date: ____________________

Review Units 7 - 9

Unit 7 から Unit 9 までの復習

►Practice 2 Feelings Quiz どんな気持ち？ 62

A. Circle the answers for the questions that are true for you.

質問を読み、自分の答えに合う絵を選び、記号を丸で囲みましょう。

1. What is the scariest?

a) Ghosts

b) Roller coasters*

c) Snakes

d) Spiders

2. What is the most exciting?

a) Amusement parks*

b) Dancing

c) Karaoke

d) Sports

e) Concerts

3. What is the most stressful*?

a) A difficult class

b) Giving a speech

c) A lot of homework

d) Being late

4. What makes you the happiest?

a) Getting a present

b) Getting a good grade*

c) Getting social media likes and comments*

d) Winning a prize* or game

5. What makes you the angriest?

a) A loud* person

b) Young people not giving a seat

c) Someone telling a lie*

d) Someone gossiping* about you

e) Online bullying* (cyberbullying)

*roller coaster ジェットコースター　amusement park 遊園地　stressful ストレスの多い
grade 成績　comments コメント　prize 賞　loud うるさい
tell a lie うそをつく　gossip うわさ話をする　bullying いじめ

B. Talk about your answer for Part A, as shown below: 63

上記で表した色々なものに対する自分の気持ちを、例を参考にして以下のようにまとめてみましょう。

Example: I will talk about my feelings about different things. Snakes are the scariest. I think amusement parks are the most exciting. Giving a speech is the most stressful. Getting a present makes me the happiest. Online bullying makes me the angriest.

Unit 10
Communication
コミュニケーション

Speaking スピーキング

Practice the following dialogues with a partner. After you have practiced the model conversation a few times, substitute the underlined information with the words in the boxes.
以下の会話をパートナーと練習してください。数回練習したら、下線の部分を枠内の表現に言いかえて再度練習しください。

Dialogue 1 64

Mike: Hi. I'm Mike. Mike Miller. And you are...(1)?

Yui: I'm Yui Takahashi. (It's) Nice to meet you.

Mike: Say, Yui, you're Japanese, right*?

Yui: Yeah. I live in Tokyo. And you?

Mike: I'm American, but I live in Japan. I live in Yokohama. I study Japanese.

Yui: Oh, really(2)?

1. And your name is ...?	2. Oh, is that right?

*right? ～だよね？

Dialogue 2 65

Yui: I'm a university student. I study nursing.

Mike: Oh, really?

Yui: I want to be a nurse in America in the future.

Mike: Good for you*(1)! I want to study at a university in Japan next year.

Yui: Wow! That's wonderful.(2)

Mike: Yeah, but I need to learn more Japanese first.

Yui: Well, good luck.

1. Oh, great!	2. interesting

*good for you よくできたね！

▶Practice 1 Listening リスニング 66

Listen to two conversations. Which one is the best? Why?

会話を聞いてください。どちらがより良い会話だと思いますか？それはなぜですか？

▶Practice 2 Matching あいづちの意味

Put the correct letters for the answers in the space.

1～10の表現を最も適切に説明する文をA～Jの中から選びましょう。

______	1. Uh-huh.	A. I understand.
______	2. I see.	B. That's correct*.
______	3. Um ...	C. What did you say?
______	4. Wow!	D. That's unbelievable.
______	5. Oh, no! That's awful*.	E. Yes. I'm listening.
______	6. Oops!	F. Just a moment*.
______	7. No way!	G. I'm surprised.
______	8. That's right.	H. I'm thinking.
______	9. Hold on.	I. That's terrible*!
______	10. Sorry?	J. I made a mistake*.

*correct 正しい　awful ひどい　Just a moment ちょっと待って
terrible ひどい　make a mistake ミスをする

Culture Note

During a conversation, silence is often not positive in many English-speaking countries. There are words and sounds you can make to show you are listening and are interested. You can see some of the common conversation responses in Practice 2 and Practice 3.

英語圏や欧米の文化では、会話の中の沈黙はあまりポジティブに受け取られないことがあります。相手の話を聞いているか、興味を持っているのかどうかは、あいづち（言葉や音声）で表せます。Practice 2 と Practice 3 で、よく使われるあいづちを見てみましょう。

▶Practice 3 Writing 適切なあいづちをさがそう 67

Look at the responses in the box below. Choose a response for each statement.

1～8のコメントや質問に対する最も適切な受け答えを、枠内から選びましょう。

Oh, is he? I'm sorry to hear that.	That's fantastic*! Do you have her picture?	
Sounds great.* I'd love to.	Oh, did I? I'm sorry.	No way! You're kidding.*
Oops! Thanks for telling me.	That's too bad. Are you OK?	Me, too. Let's go!

Statement	Reply
1. I have a new girlfriend.	______________________
2. My grandfather is sick.	______________________
3. You dropped* some money.	______________________
4. I won $1,000,000 in the lottery*.	______________________
5. Would you like to see a baseball game?	______________________
6. I'm ready to go*.	______________________
7. I think I hurt* my leg.	______________________
8. You stepped* on my toes.	______________________

* fantastic すばらしい　(It) Sounds great. すばらしい　kidding 冗談を言う　drop 落とす
lottery 宝くじ　be ready to (go)（行く）準備ができている　hurt 痛める　step 踏む

▶Practice 4 Matching 適切なあいづちをさがそう

Put the correct letters for the answers in the spaces.

AとBの質問やコメントに対するもっとも適切な受け答えを、それぞれA～Eの中から選んびましょう。

A.

______ 1. Sorry, what's your first name again?

______ 2. I got 100 on the test.

______ 3. Our dog, Fifi, died yesterday.

______ 4. We have a test tomorrow, right?

______ 5. I have a job interview* tomorrow.

A. Great! Good luck!

B. Oh, no! I'm sorry to hear that.

C. It's Mike.

D. Congratulations*!

E. We do? I forgot all about it.

B.

______ 1. You're late. What happened*?

______ 2. We have a lot of homework. I can't keep up*.

______ 3. My brother shouts* at me when he's angry.

______ 4. Are you ready* to go?

______ 5. Thank you for your help.

A. Don't worry about it. I'll help you.

B. That's not very nice of him.

C. Sorry. My train was late.

D. Just a minute.

E. Sure. Don't mention it*.

*job interview 仕事の面接　Congratulations おめでとう　What happened? どうしたの？
keep up ついていく　shout 叫ぶ　be ready (to go) もう行ける　Don't mention it 気にしないで

▶Practice 5 Nonverbal Communication 非言語コミュニケーション

Match the communication expressed in the pictures by putting the correct letters (A-O) before the expressions on page 110.

以下の絵は何を伝えようとしているのでしょうか？ 1～15の英語表現を表す絵をA～Oの中から選びましょう。

A.

B.

C.

D.

E.

F.

G.

H.

I.

J.

K.

L.

M.

N.

O.

_____ 1. Good luck.

_____ 2. I can't hear.

_____ 3. Perfect*!

_____ 4. I don't know.

_____ 5. Stop!

_____ 6. A little.

_____ 7. It's stinky*.

_____ 8. Love.

_____ 9. Oh, no! I forgot.

_____ 10. Oops!

_____ 11. Come here.

_____ 12. Yuck*!

_____ 13. Shh*!

_____ 14. Yay!

_____ 15. Ouch*!

*perfect 最高の、完璧な　stinky 臭い　Yuck! ゲー！　Shh! しー！　Ouch! いたい！

▶Practice 6 Reading リーディング 68

Nonverbal Communication
非言語コミュニケーション

Many people think that communication is just speaking with words. But communication is more than that. We change our voices* to show feeling and to make our communication more interesting. Sometimes our voices go up and down, which is called "intonation*." We say certain* words louder*, which is called "stress." We also speak with our bodies, which is called "nonverbal communication." We make hand gestures, change the expressions* on our faces, have eye contact*, and move our bodies in different ways to communicate a message or feeling. We also sometimes make different noises* to show our feelings or show that we are listening to someone.

When we move to other cultures and countries, the language we hear is usually different. Nonverbal communication also changes. These changes make communication with foreigners* difficult, so we often make mistakes.

* voice 声　intonation 発音の抑揚、イントネーション　certain ある特定の　louder より大きな声（音）で　expression 表現　eye contact 視線を合わせること　noise 雑音、不快な音　foreigner 外国人

True or False 内容把握

Write "T" for true or "F" for false for each of the sentences below.
内容と一致している場合は "T"、一致していなければ "F" を入れましょう。

______ 1. We communicate using words only.

______ 2. We make communication more interesting by changing our voices.

______ 3. "Stress" is the same as "intonation."

______ 4. Communication with our bodies is called "nonverbal communication."

______ 5. Eye contact is a part of nonverbal communication.

______ 6. The noises we make usually have no meaning.

______ 7. Nonverbal communication is the same all over the world.

▶Practice 7 Gesture Game ジェスチャーゲーム

Your teacher will give you some words to act out nonverbally. Try your best and have fun!

先生が感情を表す表現をあなたに教えます。その単語を言葉を使わずに体や表情を使って表してみましょう。楽しみながらゲーム感覚でやってみましょう。

Grammar 3

69

Present Continuous Tense (with "wh" questions and answers)

現在進行形（"Wh" を使った質問と答え）

What are you doing?	I'm doing my homework.
What's he doing?	He's working.
What's she doing?	She's talking on the phone.
Where are they going?	They're going home.
Why's she leaving?	She has an appointment* with a friend.
Who's having a birthday party?	Greg is (having a birthday party).

*appointment 約束

▶Practice 8 What Is He Doing? 彼は今何をしていますか？

Write answers to the questions, referring to the pictures. Sometimes you must use your imagination! Write in complete sentences.

絵に関する質問に、完全な文で答えてください。想像力を使いましょう！

Example: What is he doing?
He is playing the guitar.

1. What is she studying?

______________________________.

2. What sport are they playing?

______________________________.

3. What are they making?

______________________________.

4. Who is driving?

______________________________.

5. What are they playing?

______________________________.

6. What are they talking about?

______________________________.

▶Practice 9 Find the Differences 違いを探そう

Student A: Look at the picture below. **Student B:** Look at the picture in **Appendix 7**. Tell your partner what is happening in each picture. Find eight differences between your picture and your partner's.

Student A は以下の絵を見てください。Student B は Appendix 7 の絵を見てください。パートナーにお互い自分の見ている絵を説明し、違いを 8 つ見つけましょう。

Student A

Jun

Examples:

Student A: In my picture, Jun's playing tennis.

Student B: It's different. In my picture, Jun's tying* his shoes.

Student B

Jun

Student A

Franco Teruo

Student A: In my picture, Franco and Teruo are playing soccer.

Student B: It's the same. In my picture, Franco and Teruo are also playing soccer.

Student B

Franco Teruo

* tie 結ぶ

Student A

1.

Megan

2.

Ami

3.

Tony

4.

Yutaro

5.

Emma

6.

Sarah

7.

Ted

8.

Jayden

9.

Taka and Eika

10.

Lisa

Unit 11

Memories

想い出

Speaking スピーキング

Practice the following dialogues with a partner. After you have practiced the model conversation a few times, substitute the underlined information with the words in the boxes.

以下の会話をパートナーと練習してください。数回練習したら、下線の部分を枠内の表現に言いかえて再度練習しください。

Dialogue 1 70

Ben: Where did you go to high school?

Gen: I went to a school in Karuizawa.

Ben: Did you enjoy your high school days(1)?

Gen: Yes, I did.(2) I had a great time there.

Ben: What did you like about it?

Gen: I liked playing badminton the best.(3)

1. Was it a good school	2. Yes, it was	3. most

Dialogue 2 71

Taku: How was your weekend, Diane?

Diane: It was OK.(1) I had a lot of homework, so I studied a lot. How about you(2)?

Taku: I went shopping with my friends. I bought some clothes. I'm wearing them now.

Diane: You look great! Where did you go shopping?

Taku: We went to Shibuya. After shopping, we went to my favorite restaurant.(3)

1. Not bad	2. And you	3. coffee shop

Grammar 1

72

Past Tense

過去形

What ***did*** you do last weekend?	I ***went*** shopping with my friends.
What ***did*** you buy?	I ***bought*** some shoes.
How ***was*** your vacation?	It ***was*** wonderful.
Where ***did*** you go on vacation?	I ***went*** to Hawaii.
Why ***didn't*** you come to school yesterday?	I ***was*** sick.
When ***did*** you enter* university?	(I ***entered*** it) Two years ago.

* enter 入る、入学する

Grammar 2

Past Tense

過去形

There are two kinds of past-tense verbs, regular and irregular. For most regular verbs, simply add "ed" to the end of the verb (i.e. walk→walk**ed**). With verbs that end in a "y", like worry, the "y" is dropped and "ied" is added (i.e. worry → worr**ied**).

動詞の過去形には、規則変化する動詞と不規則変化する動詞があり、規則変化の過去形には、以下の二つがあります。

① 動詞の現在形に ed を付ける　walk → walk**ed**

② y で終わる動詞の場合は、y を取って ied を付ける。worry → worr**ied**

▶Practice 1　Past Tense　過去形

Write the simple past of the following verbs. The first one has been done for you.

以下の動詞の過去形を書いてください。

Regular Verbs 規則変化する動詞

Present Tense 現在形	Past Tense 過去形	Present Tense 現在形	Past Tense 過去形
1. arrive	*arrived*	7. move	______
2. carry	______	8. save	______
3. chase	______	9. study	______
4. hate	______	10. walk	______
5. hurry	______	11. want	______
6. like	______	12. worry	______

Irregular Verbs 不規則変化する動詞

Present Tense 現在形	Past Tense 過去形	Present Tense 現在形	Past Tense 過去形
1. be	*was*	10. go	____________
2. bring	____________	11. have	____________
3. buy	____________	12. leave	____________
4. come	____________	13. ride	____________
5. do	____________	14. run	____________
6. drink	____________	15. see	____________
7. eat	____________	16. spend	____________
8. fly	____________	17. take	____________
9. get	____________	18. wear	____________

▶Practice 2 Fill in the Blanks: Irregular Verbs 穴埋め問題：不規則変化の動詞の過去形

Change the sentences to the simple past.

以下の文章を過去形に変えてください。

Example:

Kenji likes to swim.
He ***swam*** in the hotel pool this morning.

1. I go to the university five days a week.
I ____________ to the university yesterday.

2. Nami usually studies in the evening.
She ____________ all night on Sunday.

3. Sid almost always* buys cheap* clothes, but yesterday he ____________ an expensive* suit.

4. Hinata usually eats at home, but she ____________ at a restaurant on Friday.

5. Kate usually sees her friends at school.
   She ___________ them yesterday, too.

6. I often meet my best friend.
   I ___________ her again two days ago.

7. My mom often makes lunch for me.
   She ___________ lunch for me again today.

8. Mike takes a train to work.
   He ___________ a train to work this morning.

* almost always ほとんどいつも　cheap 安い　expensive 高い

Grammar 4

Phrasal Verbs

二語動詞（句動詞）

Phrasal verbs are made of two or more words to create a new meaning.
二語動詞とは、二つの単語（一つは動詞）を組み合わせて、新たな意味を表します。

Regular Verbs 規則変化する動詞

Present Tense 現在形	Past Tense 過去形	Meaning 意味
1. ask for	asked for	頼む
2. clean up	cleaned up	掃除する
3. look for	looked for	探す
4. pick up	picked up	迎えに行く
5. stay up	stayed up	夜遅くまで起きている
6. try on	tried on	試着する

Irregular Verbs 不規則変化の動詞

Present Tense 現在形	Past Tense 過去形	Meaning 意味
1. come back	came back	帰ってくる
2. eat out	ate out	外食する
3. fall down	fell down	倒れる
4. find out	found out	見つける
5. get on/off	got on/off	乗る / 降りる
6. get up	got up	起きる
7. give up	gave up	あきらめる
8. go back	went back	戻る、帰る
9. grow up	grew up	育つ
10. put on	put on	着る
11. sleep in	slept in	遅くまで寝ている
12. stand up	stood up	立つ
13. take off	took off	脱ぐ
14. think about	thought about	～について考える

▶Practice 3 Pair Work: Phrasal Verbs ペアワーク：二語動詞（句動詞）

Work with a partner. Read the passage below and fill in the missing words from the choices given in the box. Put the verbs in the past tense. One phrasal verb is done for you.

空欄に入る最も適切な二語動詞を枠内から選び、過去形に変えて入れましょう。

go back　try on　give up　sleep in
think about　~~find out~~　get up
eat out　get on　look for

My sister and I went shopping on Saturday. We ____________ the train and went to Harajuku. We ____________ Gara Fashions using GPS. When we got there*, we ____________ different clothes and shoes. I liked one dress a lot, so I ____________ buying it. However, I ***found out*** it was really expensive, so I ____________. After shopping, we ____________ at a nice restaurant.

We ____________ home late on Saturday night. I ____________ on Sunday morning. I ____________ at 11 a.m.

* get there その場所に着く

▶Practice 4 Writing: Past Tense ライティング：過去形

Write answers to the following questions using full sentences.

以下の質問に、完全な文で答えてください。

Example: A: What did you do on your last birthday?
B: ***I had a birthday party with my family.***

1. What did you do last Saturday? ____________________
2. Did you sleep in on Sunday? ____________________
3. What time did you get up? ____________________
4. Where did you go on your last vacation? ____________________
5. Did you eat out last week? ____________________
6. Who did you sit next to in class yesterday? ____________________
7. Where did you leave your smartphone last night? ____________________
8. Did you watch TV last night? ____________________
9. What time did your first class begin today? ____________________
10. What did you last buy at a convenience store? ____________________
11. How much did it cost*? ____________________
12. How much money did you spend* yesterday? ____________________

* cost（お金などが）かかる　spend（お金や時間を）使う

Now ask the questions to your partner.

では、あなたのパートナーに同じ質問をしてみましょう。

▶Practice 5 Pair Work: Running Dictation ペアワーク：ストーリーゲーム

You are now going to do a running dictation. Listen carefully to your teacher's instructions and have fun in this contest. Number 1 and 6 have already been done for you. Good luck.

ストーリーゲームです。先生の説明をよく聞いて、このゲームを楽しみましょう。1と6はすでに記入されています。

Key Words

finish 終わる　call someone's name 誰かの名前を呼ぶ
scream 叫ぶ　run away 逃げる

Number:

1. ***Kana is a university student. She had classes yesterday.***

6. ***No one lived there, but someone called her name.***

▶Practice 6 Find Someone Who … こんな人を探そう

First, complete the follow-up questions on the left of the chart below. Then find someone who answers "yes" to the first question and write their names on the right. After that, ask your second question and write notes about their answer. Talk to as many people as you can.

表の左側の質問文を完成させ、その質問に Yes（否定の質問で聞かれたら答えは No）と答えられる人を見つけたら、右側の欄に記入してください。できるだけ多くの人に質問しましょう。

Example: Question: Did you study last night?
Answer: Yes, I did. (Write down the person's name)
Question: What did you study?
Answer: I studied English. (Write "English" or "Studied English")

Questions	Name / Note
1. Did you study last night? What ______________________________?	
2. Did you eat breakfast this morning? What ______________________________?	
3. Did you watch TV last night? What ______________________________?	
4. Did you go somewhere last weekend? Where ______________________________?	
5. Did your mother make lunch for you this morning? What ______________________________?	
6. Were you tired last night? Why ______________________________?	

▶Practice 7 Sharing Memories 想い出をシェアする

Work in groups. You will share memories (scary, sad, happy, early) with your classmates.

グループワーク：枠内のテーマでそれぞれの想い出（怖い、悲しい、幸せな、小さい時の想い出など）をみんなでシェアしてみましょう。

A SCARY MEMORY 怖い思い出
A Sad Memory 悲しい想い出
A HAPPY MEMORY 幸せな思い出
An Early Memory 幼い時の思い出

▶Practice 8 Pair Work: Memory Challenge ペアワーク：メモリーゲーム

Look at the picture story in **Appendix 8** for two minutes. Try to remember the story. Close **Appendix 8** and then write numbers on the left to put the sentences in the correct order. Put the verbs in the past tense. Numbers 4 and 7 have already been done for you.

Appendix 8の絵を2分間見て、ストーリーをよく覚えておきましょう。テキストを閉じ、ストーリーの内容の順番を空欄に入れましょう。4と7はすでに記入されています。

Key Words

dolphin イルカ　chase away 追い払う　shark サメ　arrive 到着する
get lost 迷子になる　ocean 海　dive 潜る

Number	
	They ____________ (see) many colorful fish and other things.
	Some dolphins* ____________ (come) and ____________ (chase away*) the shark.
4.	The next day, they ***went*** (go) to the beach.
	They ____________ (arrive) at their hotel at night.
7.	The young boy ***got lost*** (get lost*), so he swam and swam to look for his family.
	A family ____________ (fly) to a tropical island for a vacation.
	The family ____________ (check in) to the hotel at the lobby.
	Two dolphins ____________ (take) the boy back to his family.
	Then the boy and his sister ____________ (ride) on the dolphins.
	Suddenly, a shark ____________ (come) and attacked him.
	They ____________ (swim) in the ocean together and they ____________ (dive) under the waves.

▶Practice 9 Listening リスニング 73

Listen to the following presentation and write in the missing words below.

以下のプレゼンテーションを聞いて空欄を埋めましょう。

Hello everybody. Today, I'd like to tell you about ________________. Last year, I had my 20th birthday. It was a school day, but when I ________________, my friends only said, "________________." I thought they ________________ was my birthday. I ______________ lonely*. I ________________ my friends. We __________________ things, but ________________ "Happy birthday."

After I finished eating, ____________________. But then I ______________________. It was the birthday song. My friends ______________ the room with a cake and a present. I was so happy. ___________________ a book they made. It ____________________ of us. It also ____________________ the times we spent* together. It was a ____________________. When ______________, I cried. I'm so lucky to have ____________________.

Thank you very much for listening.

*lonely さびしい　spend 過ごす

▶Practice 10 Presentation プレゼンテーション

Prepare a presentation about an important event or person in your life that had an impact on you. You can use some of the language in Practice 9.

自分に最も影響を与えた出来事や人物についてプレゼンテーションをしてみましょう。枠内の例や Practice 9 を参考にしてください。

Unit 12
Into the Future
未来のこと

Speaking スピーキング

Practice the following dialogues with a partner. After you have practiced the model conversation a few times, substitute the underlined information with the words in the boxes.
以下の会話をパートナーと練習してください。数回練習したら、下線の部分を枠内の表現に言いかえて再度練習しください。

Dialogue 1 74

Pat: What will you do this weekend, Reina?
Reina: I'll study for some tests.
Pat: Oh, really? What tests?
Reina: English and history*(1).
Pat: Well, don't study too hard.(2) Try to enjoy your weekend, too.

1. Math and science*	2. overdo* it

*history 歴史　math (mathematics)　science 科学　overdo やりすぎる

Dialogue 2 75

Nana: What will you do after graduation*, Rao?
Rao: I'll go back to India. I have to find a job there. And you, Nana?
Nana: I don't know yet. Maybe I'll go overseas* and study English.
Rao: Great! Will your parents pay* for that?
Nana: Maybe not. I'll have to get a part-time job and save* some money.

*graduation 卒業　overseas 海外　pay (money) 払う　save (money) 貯める

Grammar 1

76

Future Tense with "will"

"will" を使って未来を表す

I***'ll*** (I ***will***) go shopping this week.
He***'ll*** be disappointed.
She***'ll*** go home 10 minutes from now.
They***'ll*** worry about the interview.
We***'ll*** be happy to help you.
She***'ll*** study tonight.

I ***won't*** (***will not***) spend much money.
He ***won't*** be disappointed.
She ***won't*** go home now.
They ***won't*** worry about the homework.
We ***won't*** work too hard.
She ***won't*** study tomorrow night.

▶Practice 1 Feelings 気持ち

Part A

Write sentences about the feelings people will likely have when they experience certain situations. Use the adjectives in the box.

枠内の形容詞を使って、様々な状況で人がどんな気持ちになるかを想像してみましょう。

shocked　confused　scared　disappointed　tired　~~happy~~　excited

Example: She'll get an A on the English test.
She'll be happy.

1. She'll go to a concert tonight. The concert is by her favorite singer.
______________________________.
2. His grandmother is in the hospital. He doesn't know yet.
______________________________.
3. We'll watch a horror movie on TV tonight.
______________________________.
4. She'll work hard until 11 p.m. tonight.
______________________________.
5. He's getting new software for his computer. It's very difficult to understand.
______________________________.
6. They'll lose their volleyball game because the other team is too strong.
______________________________.

Part B

Now write sentences about feelings people will ***not*** have when they experience the following situations. Use the adjectives in the box.

以下の状況ではどうでしょうか？こんな気持ちにはならない、という否定の文を書いてみましょう。

nervous　　bored　　happy　　~~surprised~~

Example: Jon will have a surprise party today, but I already told him about it by mistake.
He won't be surprised.

1. Sharon will get a low score on the test.

   ______________________________.

2. Kelly will give a speech tomorrow. She loves giving speeches.

   ______________________________.

3. We'll see an exciting movie today.

   ______________________________.

Grammar 2

77

Questions and answers with "will"

"will" を使った質問と答え

What ***will*** you do after class today?	I'***ll*** go home.
What ***will*** you do this weekend?	I'***ll*** go shopping.
When ***will*** this class finish?	(It ***will*** finish) At 4:30 p.m.

▶Practice 2 Writing: Future Plans ライティング：今後の予定

Write answers to the following questions.

以下の質問に答えましょう。

1. What will you do after class today?

   ____.

2. What will you do this weekend?

   ____.

3. What time will you have dinner tonight?

   ____.

4. Where will you go on your next trip*?

   ____.

5. Who will you travel with?

   ____.

* trip 旅行

▶Practice 3 Listening リスニング 78

Listen to the dialogue and write in the missing words.

会話を聞いて空欄を埋めましょう。

Harry: ____________________, Tomomi? You ____________________.

Tomomi: ____________________. I ____________________ some tests ____________________, so ____________________ a lot.

Harry: I see. ____________________. I hope ____________________.

Tomomi: Me, too. ____________________ them.

Harry: You shouldn't ____________________. I'm sure ____________________.

Tomomi: ____________________. I have 20 classes a week now, so it's a lot of stress. ____________________ when the tests are over*.

* be over 終わる

▶Practice 4 Story ストーリー

A fortune teller* tells you about things that will happen in the future. Complete the story with the verbs from the boxes below. Two sentences have been done for you.

占い師が未来の出来事を言いあてます。以下の絵や枠内の語句を使って未来の話を作りましょう。文中の２つの空欄には、すでに単語が書き込まれています。

* fortune teller 占い師

be (4 times) fall have ~~meet~~ marry

You will ***meet*** a man next year.  He will _______ tall and handsome.*

You will _______ in love* and then, in three years, you will  ___________ him. You will _______ three children. The first child will _______ kind. The second child will _______ intelligent.* The third child will _______ good at sports.

work change be (4 times) get have help ~~lose~~ make (2 times)

Your husband will ***lose**** his job. You will _______ poor* for two years. You will _______ a job and then you will  _______ very hard. But you will _______ very successful.* You will _______ a lot of money. You will  _______ rich. But be careful, because money will not _______ you happy. You will _______ your thinking and will _______ a better person. You will  _______ many people. Then you will _______ a happy life.

* handsome ハンサムな fall in love 恋に落ちる intelligent 知的な lose なくす poor 貧しい successful 成功した

Grammar 3

Future Tenses

未来形

The two future tenses are made with "will" and "be going to." They are often interchangeable. However, there are times that only "will" can be used.

未来形を表すには、will と be 動詞＋ going to ＋動詞の原形という2つの表し方があります。ほとんどの場合、どちらでも使えますが、例外もあります。

Will / Be going to (both used when there is a plan)　すでに前もって予定していた行動

A: What ***will*** you ***do*** this summer vacation?
B: I ***will*** *go* to Karuizawa with my family.

or

A: What ***are you going to do*** this summer vacation?
B: I'***m going to go*** to Karuizawa with my family.

Will (used when there is no plan ahead of time or when a person is not sure about future plans)　特に予定していないか、その場で即座にやろうと決めた行動

I'm thirsty.*　I'***ll*** get you some water, then.
When will we finish this homework?　I'm not sure. Maybe we'***ll*** finish in about 30 minutes.
I'***ll*** help you with your homework if you want.

* thirsty　のどが渇いた

▶Practice 5　Pair Work　ペアワーク

Imagine you are a fortune teller. You will tell the fortune of a person in your class. Write six sentences like the sentences in Practice 4. Use both "will" and "going to."

あなたが占い師だと想定してください。クラスメイトを占います。練習４で作った文を参考に、"will" か "be going to" を使って文を６つ考えましょう。

1. ______________________________.
2. ______________________________.
3. ______________________________.
4. ______________________________.
5. ______________________________.
6. ______________________________.

▶Practice 6 What Will Happen? これから何をする？

Complete the sentences below using the verbs in the box. Use the pictures as hints. Use "going to" for situations where there is a plan and "will" for times when the plan is uncertain or made suddenly.

絵をみて枠内の単語を使い、これからすることについて文を書きましょう。"be going to" はすでに予定していた行動に対して、"will" はその時突然決めた行動に対して使います。

~~visit~~ look for* have sleep go get ~~watch~~ study

* look for～ ～を探す

Examples:

Maybe I will watch TV tonight.

We are going to visit our grandparents this weekend.

1. **Ron:** I'm thirsty!
   Nonoka: OK, then I ________________ you some juice.

2. We ________________ to Hawaii this summer! We bought tickets yesterday.

3. **Sid:** What are you going to do on Sunday?
   Sheri: Maybe I ________________ all day. I'm so tired.

4. **Eric:** Can you come to the party this Friday?
   Momoko: Sorry, but I ________________ a test on Saturday, so I ________________ for it on Friday.

5. Oh, no! I lost* my key. I ______________________ it now.

* lost なくす (lose) の過去形

▶Practice 7 Pair Work: Travel Plans ペアワーク：旅行の計画 79

Student A: Look at this page. **Student B:** Look at **Appendix 9.** First, read the example questions below. Then, look at charts 1 to 4. Ask questions to find out the missing information.

Student A はこのページの情報を見て、Student B は、Appendix 9 を見てください。空欄に欠けている情報を書き入れましょう。

Example:	Questions	Answers
Destination*:	Where will Jun go on vacation*?	(He'll go to) Rome.
Date of departure*:	When will he leave?	(He'll leave on) July 4th.
Transportation*:	How's he going to get there?	(He's going to get there) By plane.
Length of stay:	How long is he going to stay there?	(He's going to stay there for) Two weeks.
Activities:	What will he do there?	(He'll) See the Colosseum and eat gelato.
	How do you spell "Colosseum"?	It's C-o-l-o-s-s-e-u-m.

* destination 行先　on vacation 休暇で　departure 出発　transportation 交通手段

1.

Name: Adam Fletcher (man)	
Destination:	
Date of departure:	August 1st
Transportation:	
Length of stay:	Four nights
Activities:	Take a boat trip on the River Seine.

2.

Name: Jay Bedi (man)	
Destination:	Kyoto
Date of departure:	
Transportation:	Train
Length of stay:	
Activities:	

3.

Name: Una Fischer (woman)	
Destination:	Sydney
Date of departure:	
Transportation:	Plane
Length of stay:	
Activities:	Take pictures with a koala.

4.

Name: Minami Ueno (woman)	
Destination:	
Date of departure:	March 10th
Transportation:	
Length of stay:	Nine days
Activities:	

▶Practice 8 Planning Your Dream Vacation 理想の休暇を計画する

You will plan a one-week trip in August. Money is no problem so you can go anywhere you want! Choose two cities you are going to visit. Plan your ideal trip on the chart below. You can do research online to make some detailed plans for your trip.

8月に1週間の旅行に行きます。行きたい町(市)を2か所選び、例を参考に以下のチャートに理想の旅行を計画してください。インターネットを使ってリサーチし、詳しい計画を立ててみましょう。

Example:

August 1st	Fly from Japan to Rome, Italy.
August 2nd	Go to some famous places, such as the Trevi Fountain and the Pantheon.
August 3rd	Go shopping in Rome. Buy some clothes. Eat at Pizza Zizza restaurant.
August 4th	Go to Venice by train. Walk around the city. Walk over the Rialot Bridge. Eat at the Riviera restaurant by the sea.
August 5th	Go on a city tour. See famous places, such as Saint Mark's, a famous church.*
August 6th	Ride on a gondola.* Go shopping for gifts.
August 7th	Return to Japan.

August 1st	
August 2nd	
August 3rd	
August 4th	
August 5th	
August 6th	
August 7th	

* church 教会　gondola（イタリア・ベニスの）ゴンドラ

▶Practice 9 Pair Work: Talking about Your Dream Vacation 80
ペアワーク：理想の休暇について話す

Using the information on the chart in Practice 8, complete the chart below. Now, take turns asking another student about their travel plans.

Practice 8で作った計画を見て、以下のチャートを完成させましょう。完成させたら、今度はクラスメイトの計画について聞いてみましょう。

Example: **Pierre**: Where will you go?
Ayami: I'll go to Rome and Venice, Italy.
Pierre: Who will you go with?
Ayami: I'll go with my sister.
Pierre: How long will you stay in each city?
Ayami: I'll stay four days in Rome and three days in Venice.
Pierre: What will you do in Rome?
Ayami: We'll go to the Trevi Fountain and the Pantheon.
Pierre: What will you do in Venice?
Ayami: We'll go on a gondola.
Pierre: Will you buy anything?
Ayami: Yes, I'll buy some gifts for my family members.

Questions	Answers
Where will you go?	
Who will you go with?	
How long will you stay in each city?	
What will you do in (City 1)?	
What will you do in (City 2)?	
Will you buy anything? What will you buy?	

▶Practice 10 Listening: Dream Vacation リスニング：理想の休暇 81

Listen to the presentation about a dream vacation and write in the missing words.

理想の休暇についての発表を聞いて空欄を埋めましょう。

Hello everyone. ______________ about my dream vacation. My friend and I ______________ California for one week. ______________ Los Angeles on August 1st, and then we'll ______________ hotel. On August 2nd and 3rd, we'll go to Disneyland. I'm ______________ on many rides* there. On August 4th, ______________ Hollywood. Maybe ______________ famous actor. On August 5th, ______________ San Francisco. We'll ______________ in Chinatown and ______________ Golden Gate Bridge. We'll ______________ near Union Square. I ______________ some gifts for my family. ______________ Scoma's, a restaurant that's famous for seafood. We'll ______________ on August 7th. Thank ______________.

* ride（遊園地などの）乗り物

▶Practice 11 Presentation: Dream Vacation プレゼンテーション：理想の休暇

Prepare and give a presentation about your dream vacation. You can use the information you wrote in Practice 8 and 9 and the example presentation in Practice 10 as a model. Write eight to ten sentences.

自分が思い描く理想の休暇についてのプレゼンテーションを準備します。自分が Practice 8, 9 に書いた情報と、Practice 10 のプレゼンテーションの例を参考に、8 文から 10 文書いてみましょう。

▶Practice 1 Crossword クロスワード

Work in pairs. **Student A:** Look at this page. **Student B:** Turn to **Appendix 10**. Give hints to help your partner guess the words that you can see in your half of the crossword. But do not say the actual words in your hints. Then listen to your partner and write in the words that he / she is describing.

ペアになって，Student A はこのページを，Student B は Appendix 10 を見てください。それぞれのクロスワードですでに埋まっている単語をパートナーにあててもらいます。ヒントを出し合い，お互いのクロスワードの空欄を埋めましょう。答えを言ってしまわないように気を付けて。

Example: A: What's 1 down?
B: It's a word that means the day after today.
A: Is it "tomorrow"?
A: That's right! Now, what's 2 across?
B: It's a feeling word. Maybe you feel this before a big test.
A: I know! It's "nervous"?
B: Very good!

Student A

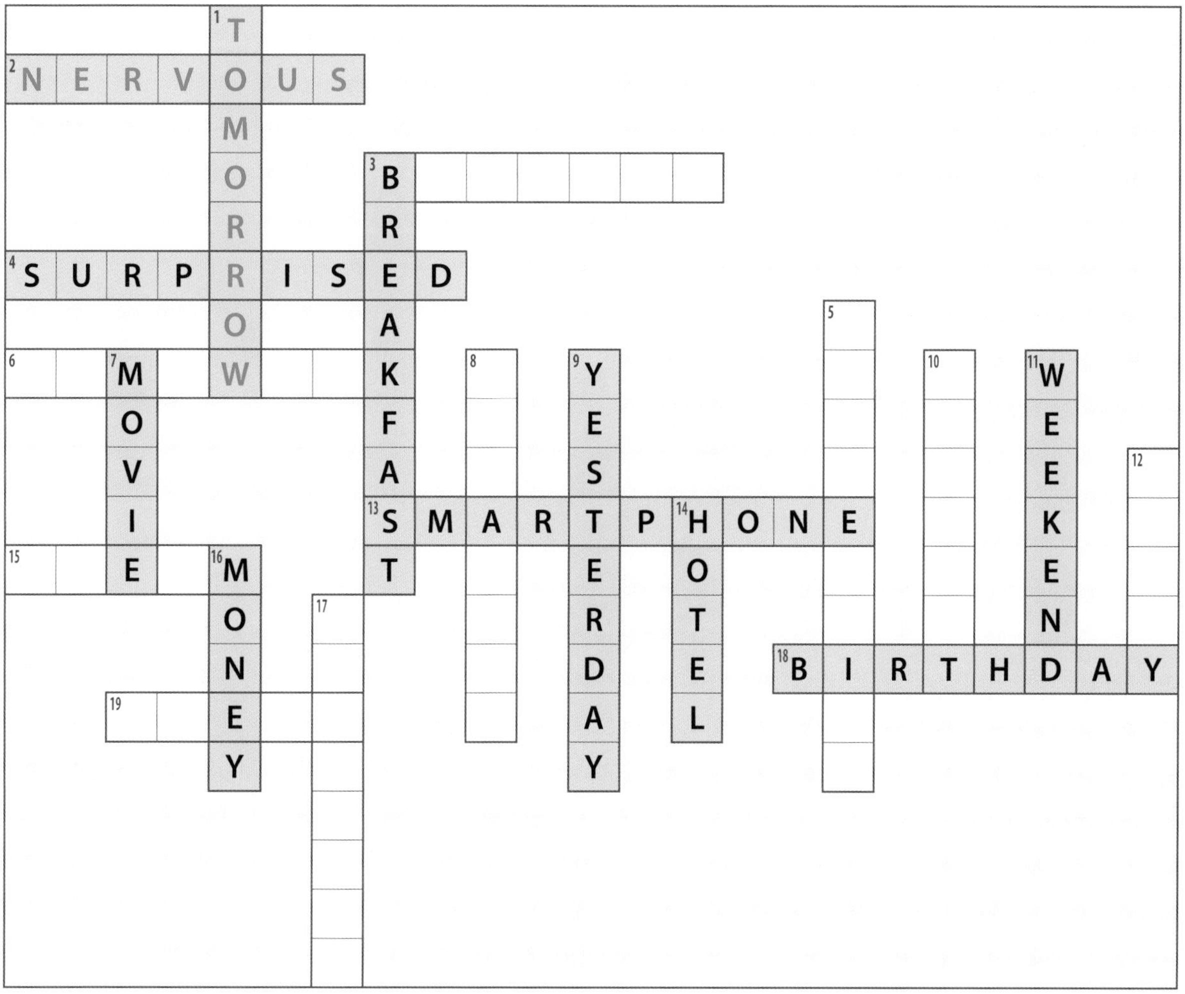

Review Units 10 - 12 Unit 10 から Unit 12 までの復習

►Practice 3 Board Game ボードゲーム

To play the board game below, you will need to make groups. Follow the instructions.
以下のルールに従って、グループでボードゲームをしてみましょう。

1. Use small pieces of paper with your initials on them as markers.
   小さな紙に自分のイニシャルを書き，自分のコマにします。
2. Toss a coin or play 'rock, paper, scissors' to decide who goes first.
   コイン使って（またはジャンケンで）誰から始めるかを決めます。

START HERE

1. What are you doing?

2. What's your teacher doing?

3. What are you studying?

4. Who are you sitting next to?

5. Did you enjoy your high school days?

6. What sport do you like best?

7. What did you do last weekend?

8. Where did you go shopping last week?

9. What's your favorite restaurant?

10. What's your favorite TV program?

11. Where did you go on your last vacation?

12. What did you eat for dinner last night?

13. Who did you sit next to in class yesterday?

3. Each player then takes turns by tossing a coin. If the coin lands face up, move two spaces. If the coin lands face down, move one space.
順番にコインを投げ、表が出たら 2 マス、裏が出たら 1 マス進みます。
4. When you land on a space, answer the question. Answer any follow-up questions.
出たマスの質問に答え，追加の質問にも答えます。

Useful expressions: 便利な表現：

I'll go first.　私が先にやります。　Is it my turn?　私の番ですか？　It's your turn.　あなたの番です。

22. When will you have dinner tonight?

23. Where will you go on your next vacation?

24. When will we finish this class?

GOAL!

21. What will you do this weekend?

20. What will you do after class today?

19. What time did your first class begin today?

18. When did you enter junior high school?

17. What did you bring to class today?

14. Where did you leave your smartphone last night?

15. How much money did you spend yesterday?

16. What did you last buy at a convenience store?

Appendix 1

Put the words in the box into the correct places in the triangle.

枠内の頻度を表す表現から適切なものを選び、１～９の空欄を埋めましょう。

sometimes	always	never	almost always/nearly always	
often	hardly ever	usually	rarely/seldom	occasionally

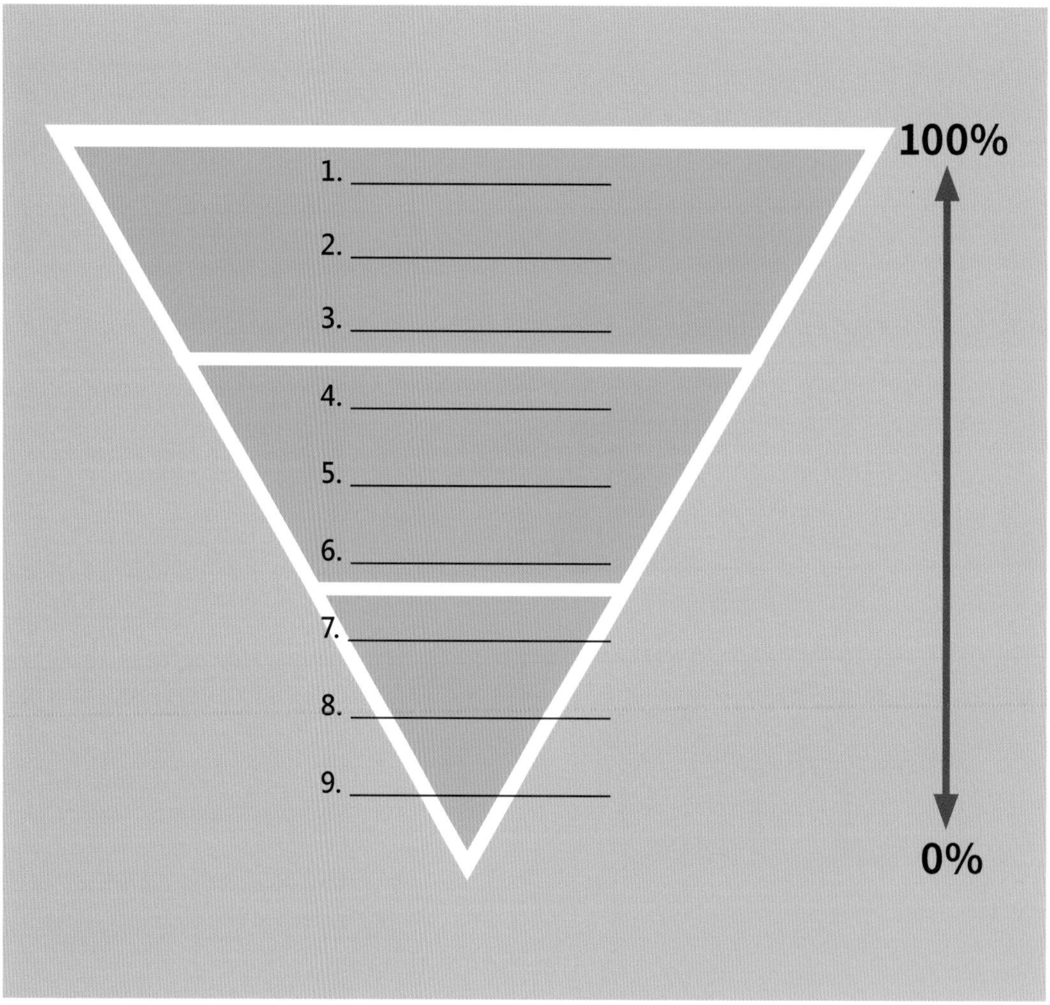

Appendix 2

Student B

Koji is a university student in Tokyo. Ask and answer questions to Student A to find the missing information in Koji's schedule.

Koji は東京の大学生です。StudentA に質問して Koji の予定の空欄を埋めましょう。

Example:

Question: What does Koji do at 6 a.m.? Answer: He wakes up (at 6 a.m.).
Question: What time does Koji wake up? Answer: (He wakes up) At 6.a.m.
Question: What does Koji do from 7:30 to 8:40 a.m.? Answer: He rides the train.

Time	Activity
6 a.m.	Koji wakes up.
	Koji eats breakfast.
7 a.m.	Koji leaves home.
7:30 a.m. – 8:40 a.m.	
8:50 a.m.	Koji arrives* at the university.
	Koji enters the classroom.
9 a.m. – 10:30 a.m.	Koji has his first class.
10:30 a.m. – 10:45 a.m.	
10:45 a.m. – 12:15 p.m.	Koji has his second class.
	Koji eats lunch.
1 p.m. – 2:30 p.m.	Koji has his third class.
2:30 p.m. – 3:30 p.m.	
3:30 p.m. – 5 p.m.	Koji studies in the library.
	Koji leaves* the university.
6 p.m. – 6:10 p.m.	Koji walks to the station.
6:10 p.m. – 7:20 p.m.	
7:25 p.m.	Koji buys food at the supermarket.
	Koji arrives home and cooks dinner.
9 p.m.	Koji watches TV.
10:30 p.m.	
11 p.m.	Koji goes to bed.

* arrive 着く　leave 出る、去る　take a shower シャワーをあびる

Appendix 3

Student B

Ask and answer questions as in the Examples to fill in the missing information for numbers 2 and 4.
以下の例を参考にして質問し、2と4についての情報を空欄に記入しましょう。

Examples:

What's his/her name?
How old is she/he?
What does she/he do?
Where does she/he live?
What does she/he do in her/his free time?
How do you spell that?
Pardon?

1

Name: Chen Li
Age: 23
Job: Model
Where / live: Shanghai
Free time: Goes shopping

2

Name: ______
Age: ______
Job: ______
Where / live: ______
Free time: ______

3

Name: Siti Imran
Age: 21
Job: Student
Where / live: Penang
Free time: Plays badminton

4

Name: ______
Age: ______
Job: ______
Where / live: ______
Free time: ______

Appendix 4

Student B

Take turns and ask questions and write down the answers in the blanks below, as shown in the example.

交代でお互いに質問をし、空欄に正しい国名、言語を入れましょう。

Example: Student A: Where is Li from?
Student B: She's from China.
Student A: How do you spell "China"?
Student B: "C-H-I-N-A." What's her nationality*?
Student A: She's Chinese. What language does she speak?
Student B: She speaks Chinese.

* nationality 国籍

Name	Country	Nationality	Language
1. Li (she)	*China*	*Chinese*	*Chinese*
2. Jules (she)	*France*	________	*French*
3. Antonio (he)	________	*Spanish*	*Spanish*
4. Kristine (she)	________	*Filipino*	________
5. Trang (he)	________	*Vietnamese*	________
6. Lucas (he)	*Canada*	________	*English and French*
7. Jack (he)	*America*	________	*English*
8. Rie (she)	________	________	*Japanese*

Appendix 5

Student B

Give hints to help your partner guess the words that you can see in your half of the crossword. But do not say the actual words in your hints. Then listen to your partner and write in the words that he / she is describing.
それぞれのクロスワードですでに 埋まっている単語をパートナーにあててもらいます。ヒントを出し合い，お互いのクロスワードの空欄を埋めましょう。 答えを言ってしまわないように気を付けて。

Example: A: What's 2 down?
B: It's a word for a family member. Your mother's daughter is your …?
A: "Sister"?
A: That's right! Now, what's 1 across?
B: It's the part of your body you use to see.
A: Is it "eyes"?
B: Yes. Well done!

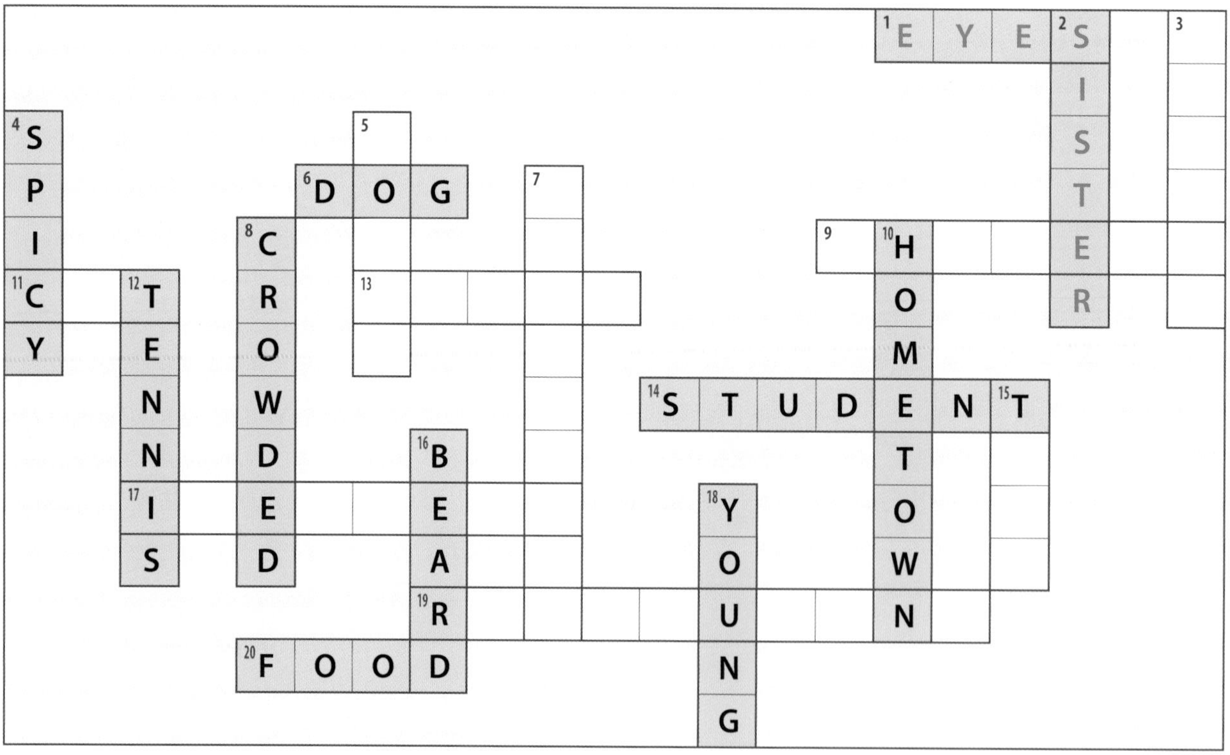

Appendix 6

Family Tree (2) 家系図（2）

Student B

There are 11 differences in Trevor's family tree. Ask questions to each other to find the differences.
お互いが見ている Trevor の家系図には 11 か所異なる点があります。パートナーに質問しながら違いを見つけましょう。

Examples: Who is Janice married to? What does Trevor do?
How old is Richard's wife? What's Richard's wife's name?

* retired 退職者　lawyer 弁護士

Appendix 7

Student B

Tell your partner what is happening in each picture. Find eight differences between your picture and your partner's.

パートナーにお互い自分の見ている絵を説明し、違いを８つ見つけましょう。

Student A

Jun

Examples:

Student A: In my picture, Jun's playing tennis.
Student B: It's different. In my picture, Jun's tying his shoes.

Student B

Jun

Student A

Franco Teruo

Student A: In my picture, Franco and Teruo are playing soccer.
Student B: It's the same. In my picture, Franco and Teruo are also playing soccer.

Student B

Franco Teruo

1. 

Megan

2. 

Ami

3. 

Tony

4. 

Yutaro

5. 

Emma

6. 

Sarah

7. 

Ted

8. 

Jayden

9. 

Taka and Eika

10. 

Lisa

Appendix 8

1.

2.

3.

4.

5.

6.

7.

8.

9.

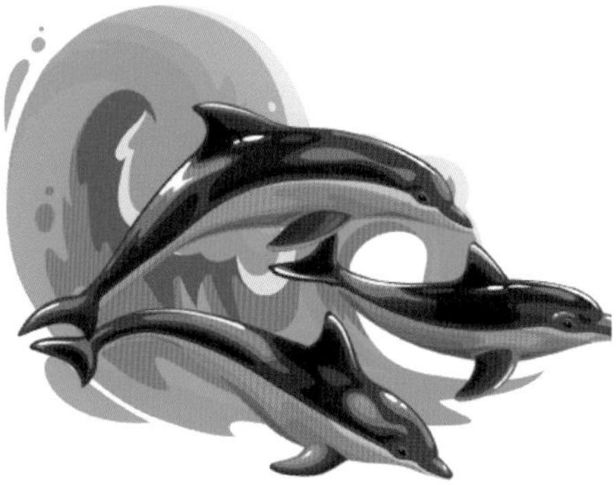

10.

11.

Appendix 9

Student B

Ask and answer questions to complete the missing information about Adam's, Jay's, Una's and Minami's travel plans.

Adam, Jay, Una, Minami の旅行計画についてお互いに質問し合い、空欄に欠けている情報を書き入れましょう。

Example:	Questions	Answers
Destination*:	Where will Jun go on vacation?	(He'll go to) Rome.
Date of departure*:	When will he leave?	(He will leave on) July 4th.
Transportation*:	How's he going to get there?	(He's going to get there) By plane.
Length of stay:	How long is he going to stay there?	(He's going to stay there for) Two weeks.
Activities:	What will he do there?	(He'll) See the Colosseum and eat gelato.
	How do you spell Colosseum?	It's C-o-l-o-s-s-e-u-m.

* destination 行先　departure 出発　transportation 交通手段

1.

Name: Adam Fletcher (man)	
Destination:	Paris
Date of departure:	
Transportation:	Ferry* and train
Length of stay:	
Activities:	

2.

Name: Jay Bedi (man)	
Destination:	
Date of departure:	July 2nd
Transportation:	
Length of stay:	One week
Activities:	Visit some famous temples*.

3.

Name: Una Fischer (woman)	
Destination:	
Date of departure:	December 22nd
Transportation:	
Length of stay:	Two weeks
Activities:	

4.

Name: Minami Ueno (woman)	
Destination:	San Francisco
Date of departure:	
Transportation:	Plane
Length of stay:	
Activities:	See the Golden Gate Bridge.

* ferry フェリー　temple お寺

Appendix 10

Crossword Puzzle

Student B

Give hints to help your partner guess the words that you can see in your half of the crossword. But do not say the actual words in your hints. Then listen to your partner and write in the words that he / she is describing.

それぞれのクロスワードですでに 埋まっている単語をパートナーにあててもらいます。ヒントを出し合い，お互いのクロスワードの空欄を埋めましょう。 答 えを言ってしまわないように気を付けて。

Example: A: What's 1 down?
B: It's a word that means the day after today.
A: Is it "tomorrow"?
A: That's right! Now, what's 2 across?
B: It's a feeling word. Maybe you feel this before a big test.
A: I know! It's "nervous"?
B: Very good!

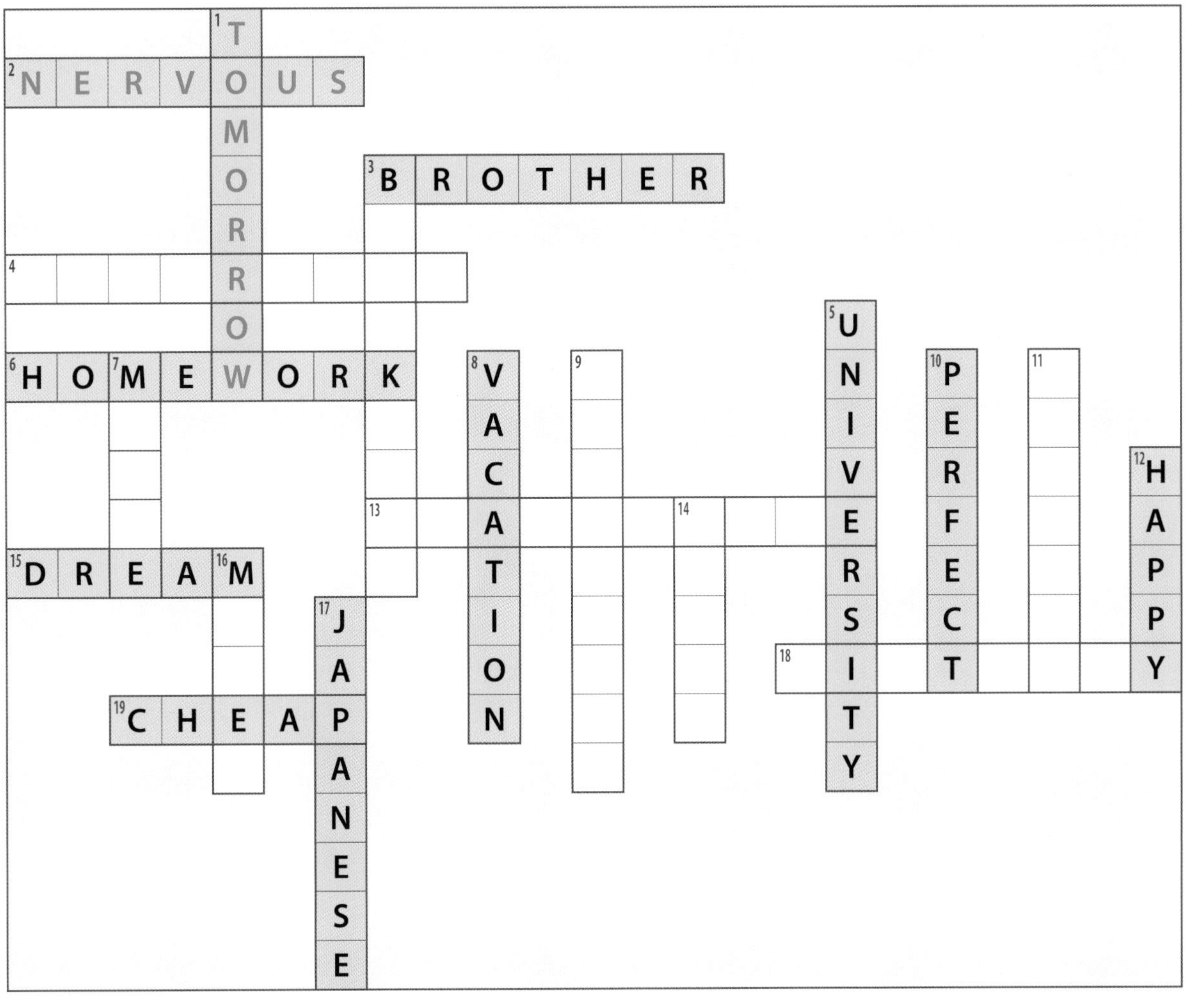

Speaking of People *Intro*
Image Credits

All photographs © Shutterstock.com except:
p. 93 © Xeravines / Shutterstock.com

Speaking of People *Intro* [B-962]
人とつながる英語コミュニケーション〔初級編〕

1 刷　2024 年 1 月 16 日

著　者　Peter Vincent　ピーター　ビンセント
Alan Meadows　アラン　メドウズ
Naoko Nakazato　中里　菜穂子

発行者　南雲一範　Kazunori Nagumo
発行所　株式会社　南雲堂
〒162-0801　東京都新宿区山吹町361
NAN’UN-DO Co., Ltd.
361 Yamabuki-cho, Shinjuku-ku, Tokyo 162-0801, Japan
振替口座: 00160-0-46863
TEL: 03-3268-2311（営業部: 学校関係）
03-3268-2384（営業部: 書店関係）
03-3268-2387（編集部）
FAX: 03-3269-2486
編集者　加藤　敦

装　丁　銀月堂
組　版　Office haru
検　印　省　略
コード　ISBN978-4-523-17962-7 C0082

Printed in Japan

E-mail nanundo@post.email.ne.jp
URL https://www.nanun-do.co.jp/